The Top 50 Most Influential Gay Movies Of All Time

JASON SHAW

This edition published 01 March 2012

© Jason Shaw 2012

All photographs, film posters, DVD covers have been reproduced faithfully from publicity material, no exertion of rights or copyright is made in respect of those images and/or artwork by Jason Shaw, either directly or indirectly. All © copyrights remain exclusive and in full with the respective film production companies/studios.

© Jason Shaw 2012 all rights reserved

This book is sold on condition that it shall not, by way of trade or otherwise, be lent, resold, hired out, or otherwise circulated without the publisher's prior consent in any form of binding or cover other than in which it was published.

ISBN 978- 1- 4710- 8645- 8

First Edition

INTRODUCTION

Hello and welcome to the very first edition of The Top 50 Most Influential Gay Movies Of All Time, I thank you for picking it up at the book store, purchasing it, downloading it to your electronic reading machine, kindle, borrowing it from a friend or even I suppose stealing it. Although I am sure, you will understand I would not recommend that last course of action! Regardless of how you came to be reading these words, I sincerely thank you for doing so and I welcome you to this, the first compendium of gay themed movies with influence.

Producing this book has been exceedingly good fun, yet it has not been without its difficulties, with the selection of movies for final consideration perhaps the biggest headache. Having been a film fan for more years than I care to remember, I already had my own personal choices, however, I wanted to open up a dialogue and hear the voices of others. For many months I blogged about it, I took to social media networks such as Twitter, Facebook, Google+ and so on. I read forums, message boards, I asked friends, I tweeted followers, and I messaged friends, friends of friends and their friends also. In fact, for a period of about seven or so months I don't think there was not a single person I encountered that I did not ask for their input, that was the fun part. I had an avalanche of suggestions, bucket loads of offerings from sources as far apart as the north of Scotland to the sunnier climbs of Sydney, Australia. There were a great many common and perhaps predictable suggestions, such as such as Brokeback Mountain and Philadelphia, yet some unusual recommendations such Threesome, The Dreamers and The History Boys. Indeed, there were numerous proposals that were as varied as the respondents themselves, which made the task of collating, calculating and condensing these suggestions into a final fifty a very difficult occupation indeed.

I'll wager that if you've got this far in the introduction in a book about influential gay movies, you'll have a favourite film, you might not believe you have one, or even admit it at first, but I bet you do, think hard and you'll find one, lurking in the back of your mind. Perhaps you have more than one, more than two, conceivably four or ten or even more, that is great it really is, it proves you watch a lot of movies and that is no bad thing. No, that is a good thing, you see watching movies is pretty much a universal occupation. Irrespective of our own personal ages, of where we come from, what social, economic or ethnic background from which we originate, one thing we can be fairly certain we have in common, is the fact or notion that we all watch movies! Some do it at home snuggled on the sofa with a loved one, some alone with a glass of wine and a box of Tesco's finest chocolates. Maybe a lone teenager or twenty-something would be streaming it from the internet in a bedroom far far away. Others do it with a group of friends usually with the accompaniment of alcohol and nibbles. Millions of others will trudge off to a big hall, or a multiple of smaller halls to enjoy these cinematic moving images of wonder dazzle before our very eyes in the company of strangers. I suppose a few of us head to the beach, or the elusive relic of yesteryear, a drive-in to enjoy these visual creations from an industry we call 'the movie'. It matters not how or where we do it, we just do it, and that is the thing you see, we do it, wherever we may be and whatever method we chose, we all do it. Film is perhaps one of the 'last' few great unifiers in this world, it transverses all borders, be they physical, political, ethnic or social, to reach out to each one of us. Films do not care if you are rich or poor, old or young, male, female or transgender, black, white, yellow or any other colour of the vast and beautiful human rainbow. You can be anyone, prince or pauper, saint or sinner, gay or straight, anything you like, the films do not care, nope, the film just reaches out to you, calling to you, asking you to view it, the rest is up to you!

Now that we have established that we are all movie watchers, the audiences of the world, the nest item on the agenda for compiling this tome was the question of what qualifies as influential. I mean that is a rather broad, subjective term open to all sorts of personal views, criteria and ideals. What may be influential to me may have no other effect, other than to induce a yawn or two on you. The Oxford English Dictionary quantifies 'influential' as 'Have the capacity to have an effect on the character, development or behaviour of someone or something'. Webster's defines it as 'Exerting or possessing influence' and influence as 'the act or power of producing an effect without apparent exertion of force or direct exercise of command'. Therefore, to apply that to film would mean we are looking at a movie or movies in the plural, that have the capacity to effect our character, development, or behaviour, which is not as hard as it may seem at first, if we allow ourselves to see character as mood. I'm sure most of us have had our moods changed by movies, we've laughed out loud at funny bits, with sniffed at slightly emotive bits and cried buckets at the heart breaking endings, or if we're warped like my friend Dean, we'd reverse those reactions and laugh out loud at the sad heart wrenching ending, or sniff at the funny bits and so on. There is little doubt, that you have found, let, allowed a movie to have an impact on your emotional state, at least for the time you were watching it, so therefore it could be argued that the movie has had some influence over your disposition and temperament. Some movies encourage us to do things, for example Days of Thunder encouraged us to all become racing drivers and 127 Hours made us all want to go and climb some rocks and cut our arms off, well maybe not that last bit, however you understand the point, some movies can make us do or think about doing something adventurous. Furthermore, there are a few films that challenge the way we think, compelling us to re-examine our beliefs or ideals and views on certain subjects, the influence they leverage is much greater and unambiguous.

Another key ingredient to calculating a films overall influence and its rightful place in this listing would be the audience factor. A wonderful world peace method film seen by one lone soul in a picture house in the back end of Basingstoke may be the most powerful film ever made with life enhancing messages in abundance. Yet with an audience of just one lonely bugger in a bobbly hat and glasses, that message is not getting out and the influence it exerts is pretty much close to the lower end of zero! Therefore, in cultivating the final fifty, I took a films audience reach into consideration, both from box office receipts, video & DVD sales, peer to peer sharing and in some cases viewing figures from television broadcastings.

Additional items into the mix of ingredients of the cake we're calling influential, beyond the audience reach came from related material, such as sequels, follow-on's, books, plays, musicals and so on. Quite often, a movie is developed from a play or a book, yet rarely does this happen in the opposite way, therefore such occasions add another level to be considered in the calculations. Other additives such as audience reactions, viewer campaigns, charity implications, watching groups, cults, fan clubs and the like were sloshed around the bowl in order to get a truly authentic and layered cake of influence.

This then is the results of that labour, the fruits of my metaphorical baking and I hope you enjoy the taste. There were some predictable and expected entries, some traditional offerings yet there were some suggestions that truly surprised me, which upon further research and reflection rightly deserved their final place in the final fifty. Another surprise was the varied age of those that responded to me and of the movies they suggested, a welcome surprise I hasten to add. You will find some modern and recent movie releases alongside older classic titles that have managed to stand the test of time and taste, remaining in the mind of the viewer a truly influential piece of film.

There may be some surprising omissions in the final fifty to some of you; either they did not quite make the final fifty due to numbers, calculations or lack of suggestions. Alternatively, it could be that they did not quite fit into the criteria of what a gay movie really is. For example, The Dreamers, whilst an excellent and cinematically supreme movie, it does not follow the book of the same name, with the gay storyline, which is completely absent from the film version, hence its exclusion from this compilation. There are a few other similar cases where movies may well have had gay characters or gay actors in supporting roles, the films themselves were not about gay people, situations or life. To be included in this compendium, I am sure you will understand it became mandatory for consideration a suggested film had to exhibit a strong gay theme along with gay central characters, I make no apology for that, otherwise, it would not have been compiling the top fifty most influential gay movies, and it would be just another top fifty films!

I sincerely hope you enjoy this little compilation, perhaps learn something new or that it goes a little way to influencing you to view a new or different movie. I am sure there will be some that would disagree with various inclusions or their position within the rankings, how could there not be? We are all different, with our own opinions, thoughts and views on what we each find enjoyable and influential, which is a great thing, however I have been faithful and honest with the suggestions and nominations received and the calculations of them to achieve their final positioning. Indeed if it had been a purely personal choice, the top ten would have been radically different!

Jason Shaw.

March 2012

50

The Fluffer

Director: Richard Glatzer, Wash West.

Starring: Scott Gurney, Michael Cunio, Roxanne Day, Taylor Negron.

The Fluffer is a rather strange and provocative introduction to the world of obsession and love in the adult entertainment industry with some painful twists along the way. It all starts when a young wide-eyed innocent film student, Sean McGinnis, played by the handsome Michael Cunio, moves to Los Angeles to try and break into the movies, like so many before him. It is not as easy as it looks in the films he rents whilst trying to get that big break. One of the movies he rents from a local video store is the classic Citizen Kane, however hapless individuals at the video rental place have somehow mixed it up with hot adult flick 'Citizen Cum'. It is this accidental mix up of tapes that gives birth to a lengthy and powerful obsession Sean develops for the porn-star star of Citizen Cum, Johnny Rebel, played perfectly by Scott Gurney.

Sean finds work on the sets of gay pornography films, first doing odd jobs, then filming and takes on the mysterious and yet sometimes highly sought after position of 'fluffer'. Now for the uninitiated the 'fluffer' is the person responsible for assisting with the performer's ability to perform, making soft things hard, in the days before Viagra!

Scott has to get hands on with porn-star Johnny Rebel and is instantly smitten with the hunk star that despite doing the deed in dozens of gay porn films is in fact straight and only gay for pay. Johnny lives with abrasive stripper girlfriend and seems to have pretty much everything. As Sean gets to know more about Johnny, whose real name outside the industry of gay porn is Mikey, he becomes more and more obsessed with the increasingly self-absorbed and utterly narcissistic star.

Tensions mount and as is often the case in tales like this, those that seem to have everything, in fact have very little, Johnny Rebel is a bit of a meth head and starts to use the drug more and more frequently. His stripper girlfriend is pregnant with his child, however, she knows that she will never be able to reply on his to provide either money or father figure for the baby, so she elects to have an abortion. It is another nail in the coffin that is Johnny

Rebel's sobriety and sanity. His ability to hold it all together is significantly compromised.

An expensive bit of kit goes missing from the studios and all eyes look towards Rebel, then one of the studios owners is found dead, murdered in his apartment and now it is the police looking toward the porn star drug addict. Could the handsome hunky star really be responsible for both crimes? Sean, does not think so and tries to make excuses for the object of his obsession, it is not a concept that most are willing to believe and you know then that yet ultimately this film is not going end with a happy ever after! Johnny pushes Sean's obsession to the maximum boundaries, taking it to the extreme limits, or Mexico as the case happens to be.

The Fluffer is an interesting film, which has surprisingly little nudity and sexy considering where the story is based. It raises many issues, such as drug abuse, corruption, obsession, self-hatred, internalized homophobia and self-discovery. It also acts as a warning against following the object of your obsession to carefully or to closely. It is not the greatest gay movie in the world, but it did perhaps open up the world of the adult entertainment industry in a slightly sanitised way that had many people talking. There were also appearances from a number of adult stars, including Chad Donovan, Thomas Lloyd, Zach Richards, Jim Steel, Chi Chi LaRue and even pop diva Debbie Harry had a small part. A surprising number of nominations helped this movie to only just creep ahead of Mambo Italiano and secure its place in the top fifty.

49

Another Gay Movie.

Director: Todd Stephens.

Starring: Michael Carbonaro, Jonathan Chase, Jonah Blechman, Mitch Morris, Graham Norton.

It had to happen at some stage, did it not? The whole American Pie larger than life lad flick feel given a coat of pink paint and a liberal dusting of glitter! Another Gay Movie is that movie. An entertaining light-hearted romp through stereotypical eyes at the lives of four teenage friends who agree to lose company with their virginity before summer's last stand. It is without a doubt one of the most outrageous gay parody films ever seen. The jokes come thick and fast and there are some that come pretty close to crossing from boundary from scandalous to bad taste. It is a silly and irreverent look at gay sexuality and lifestyles with all the exaggerations expected of a parody of this time of film. The whole plot line for example should give you all you need to know about the movie before you sit down and watch it, four gay guys desperate to lose the big V plates in a few short weeks and that is basically it. Perhaps like most spoofs the joke aspect grows thin a quarter of an hour in and the jokes just become banal and stereotypical. Camp chat show king Graham Norton takes on the role of a Russian school teacher in what is perhaps one of the most disturbing and vulgar scenes of the whole film and one has to hope he got paid a lot of money for his 'small' part. Another Gay Movie is a Marmite of a film, you will either love or hate it, for me it is the latter, but plenty more are the former and despite losing money at the box office with a take of £472,000 they still made a sequel, which was equally as daft and dull. My only hope is that the wider audience won't view this as a realistic portrayal of all gay life!

"It is simply the best gay film out there, it doesn't take itself too seriously, it sticks a finger up at the straight world as says fuck you!" **Hayden, Clapham.**

"This is your typical run of the mill teen sex story, only it is a gay version. It is so funny and had me in stitches all the way through" **Sarah, Southampton.**

"This is as funny as it gets, me and my mates love it. Direct and forceful, nice sexy actors, mild sex scenes and so many jokes my sides always hurt from laughing too much" **Stewart, Bucks.**

48

Jeffrey

Director: Chris Ashley.

Starring: Steven Weber, Patrick Stewart, Bryan Batt, Christine Baranski, Victor Garber.

Jeffrey should have been a major massive blockbuster, a sure-fire smash hit, just take a look at some of the names on the cast, Christine Baranski, Patrick Stewart, Sigourney Weaver, Kathy Najimy, Nathan Lane and Olympia Dukakis, yet it failed to set the queer or the straight world alight.

Jeffrey a gay romantic comedy from America came out in 1995/6 and was based on a Paul Rudnick play about a young gay New York guy who considers sex is too dangerous in the days of AIDS and commits to a life of celibacy. Just to throw a spanner in the works and pad the film out another hour he meets the man of his dreams, whom surprise surprise just happens to be HIV+.

It starred Steven Weber who was nice enough as the insipid Jeffrey an actor/waiter who is supposed to be AIDSaphobic, which just does not wash. Michael T. Weissis handsome and some nice eye-candy but you just wish he would get on and so something, anything as this film drags on and on and ever on. It would have been a total flop and dire mess on the floor of movie history were it not for the dozens of big names doing small cameos - Olympia Dukakis, Robert Klein, Nathan Lane, Kathy Najimy, Kevin Nealon, Ethan Phillips, Sigourney Weaver and Christine Baranski for example. For a stereotypical highlight there was a charmingly over the top performance from Patrick Stewart picking up the part of Sterling, who gets as far away from his Picard Star Trek persona as it is possible to get. Had it not been for this line up of celebs, funding and distribution would have been damn near impossible to get, considering the subject matter, a comedy about AIDS!

I may sound hard and harsh, it took a smattering over £3 million at the box office during the year of its release, a million more than it cost to make, so it must have done something right, yet for me it promised so much but just like a wet weekend in Worthing, it delivered so little.

47

Pink Narcissus

Director: James Bidgood.

Starring: Bobby Kendall.

Have little doubt, like it or loathe it, Pink Narcissus is a classic of the cult variety, lauded for its high artistic cinematic quality, position and production. It is a visual fantasia of expression, colour, eroticism, sexuality and stimulating contemporary artistry. Pink Narcissus is no shrinking violet, no wilting wallflower, it is a full on meadow in full bloom.

This low budget film took a number of years to complete and filmed, mostly, within the tight confines of writer and director James Bidgood's New York apartment. There is little in the way of plot lines or subplots, the story is as flimsy as Dick Van Dyke's accent, dialogue is virtually non-existent for this 1971 offering is all about the erotic images fostering themselves on the screen.

Bobby Kendall plays the 'kept boy' who whiles away his hours waiting for his master by dreaming of various things, he seems a young fellow obsessed with his own beauty and physical appearance, but maybe you guessed that already by the title? He envisions himself as a Turkish prince, a Roman slave, a wood nymph, a matador and even a kept boy in some far off sheiks harem. Everything is so incredulously heavy on the design front, bejewelled and stylised to excess. It is that excess, that visually expressiveness that has made this little independent movie become a landmark of gay cinema as well as a statement of contemporary art.

When the film was released, no credit was ascribed to the director, leaving that as anonymous encouraged many to speculate and cogitate on the identity of the creative master. Many of the people in the world of art and cinema were of the opinion that none other than one Mr Andy Warhol was said genius behind the camera. It was a suggestion, along with many others that continued for many years, until 1999 when it became known it was Bidgood's work after an investigation, which resulted in a small book.

Pink Narcissus remains a provocative film, not least for the pure gay erotic aspect, which treads that fine line between erotic art and pornography with blurry glasses. For many the close up ejaculation into a glass crosses that line, no matter how flickering and pink you make it. Such things still cause controversy and much discussion which ensure this hallucinogenic homoerotic narcissistic overindulgent fantasy film continues to expel some influence on the independent gay cinema scene.

"I wasn't around in the 70's but thanks to Pink Narcissus, I get a sense of being in that psychedelic decade with all its freedoms and fantasies. It is an amazing collection of horny scenes and erotic moments. I guess I'm shocked at what they could get away with back then, more than we can get away with now. Its defiantly one to be seen and enjoyed for what it is – art." **Devon, Miami.**

"I have no idea why the only speaking comes from the radio doing weather forecasts, but I suppose speaking isn't important when you have someone as pretty as Mr Kendall on screen to look at. He is so beautiful and you can easily understand why the film maker was so taken by him. If you take time to look at this film and really watch you'll see many things for the first time here that had since been used by gay artists, photographers and designers over and over again." **Bella, Shoreham.**

"No script, little plot, great visuals, a true remarkable example of influential gay movies." **Simon, London.**

46

The Sum of Us

Director: Geoff Burton, Kevin Dowling.

Starring: Russell Crowe, Jack Thompson, John Polson.

What's this, Russell Crowe playing it gay in a low budget Australian flick, could that be true? It doesn't sound like it from the surface, but digging a little deeper and that really is exactly what you have in The Sum of Us, a freakishly good low budget movie from 1994.

The Sum of Us is basically the sum of a story of looking for love, first the widowed dad is looking for love and his 'Miss Right' whilst his twentyish son is also looking for love, but in the shape of his 'Mr Right'.

This surprisingly endearing movie made on a budget less than most films spend on catering and cakes, is a witty and funny tale of love and laughter. The Sum of Us is not your typical gay movie in that nobody is dying, activism is not on the menu, nor is there a historical horror or an aggressive and overbearing father preventing the closet door from opening and not even the slightest hint of drag! Nope, this is a good and happy sort of soft tale, which has some nice funny bits and a couple of tender scenes to pique the heartstrings.

Harry Mitchell (Jack Thompson) is a wonderfully warm and giving person, he only wants the best for his son Jeff (Russell Crowe) he simply wants him to be happy. When Jeff brings home a guy, his dad Harry does everything he can to make the visitor welcome, although he does amusingly ask them if they practise safe sex. Most of the dates do not seem to understand or accept this odd and close family dynamic and do not come back to repeat the experience.

Harry think's his son's pulled a right cracker and a possible Mr Right when he brings home a handsome gardener called Greg (John Polson). There are some sweet comical moments when he keeps interrupting his sons attempts to seduce the young gardener, which puts a smile on the faces of the audience. I loved the moment he escorts Greg up to Jeff's room at one stage and offers him a couple of male gay porn mags, to help the situation along a little. He goes and leaves them to it, but only for just a moment or two before he pops back to see what Greg wants for breakfast.

Theirs is a wonderful and incredibly open father and son relationship, I bet a whole ton of gay guys would kill for, yet there has to be a little confrontation and upset, this being a movie an all. This fly in the ointment comes in the shape of Joyce, a love interest for Harry picked from a dating service. She is not exactly the warmest person when it comes to homosexuals, but that is not all, nope it's not all clear cut and happy ever after for Jeff either. His squeeze, sexy khaki short wearing gardener Greg is not 'out' and open about his sexuality, just to add an extra layer of trouble in this Aussie paradise.

The Sum of Us is taken directly from the stage play, as such, some of the lines are more 'stagey' than 'filmy' but get over those, and you have a very enjoyable film. Funny, interesting, charming, touching and rather refreshingly free from overt stereotypes, which can dog so many other gay films. It manages to retain a sense of upbeat charm and character all the way through, yes even during the slightly sad confrontational bits. Russell Crowe is incredibly fresh faced in this mid-nineties offering and is simply wonderful, you certainly see a different side to his 'acting range' and skill set here. Jack Thompson is an established actor of some repute in Australia and the onscreen connection and chemistry with Crowe is perhaps the main reason this movie works so well, believable whilst still being blokey.

"Funny, amusing, heart warmingly good. The Sum Of Us is the best and most underrated gay movie of the 90's" **Max, Weston Super Mere.**

45

The Fruit Machine

Director: Philip Saville

Starring: Emile Charles, Tony Forsyth, Robert Stephens

A beautiful, powerful and very much underrated British gritty gay thriller from the late 80's, released in the UK as The Fruit Machine and in the US as Wonderland. It is passionate, resolute, beautifully directed, filmed and played that I would have thought it would have been higher on the listing, yet here it is, languishing in the upper forties.

The Fruit Machine is a wonderful and poignant tale of growing up, it combines the rite of passage, buddy flick with a road movie genres in perfect symmetry and also shoves in a bit of a thriller just for the sake of it. BAFTA winner Philip Saville directs Emile Charles and Tony Forsyth as Eddie and Michael, two gay mates on the very brink of adulthood as they head into the adventure of their lives. These two friends may both be gay but their sexuality is the only thing they seem to have in common. In all other respects, they are as different as the proverbial chalk and cheese, Eddie is soft, gentle, sensitive and fragile. He adores nothing more than watching old classic black and white movies with his mum. Michael is much more streetwise, tough, manly and loves video games. They behave almost like an old married couple, arguing over anything at the drop of a pin, yet you can tell there is a very deep bond between them. They seek an escape from the gritty hard harsh realities of Liverpool's depressive streets. They find that escape in the fantastical and gingham check world of a drag/transvestite club called 'The Fruit Machine' run by the wonderful Annabelle, played by the superb Robbie Coltrane. The Fruit Machine could have been their salvation, had they not stumbled upon a gangland murder at the club and fearing for their lives they make a run for it. Now, where are two young gay boys going to run to when in trouble? Brighton.

Michael, the streetwise one, arranges transport and a place to stay, by selling himself and Eddie, although Eddie remains fairly unaware of that aspect of life on the run. In fact Eddie remains fairly dreamy throughout the whole film, practical things are not really his bag of spanners. He becomes a little obsessed with a completely soaking wet man he seems to see everywhere. This is the Dolphin Man played by the mysterious Carsten Norgaard, and has an immense impact on him down in Brighton, where he sneaks in and swims with the Dolphins in the SeaLife centre.

The dream of a happy fun life down by the sea on the south coast comes to a crashing colliding halt when the vicious gangland thugs from up north catch up with the runaway teens. There follows a touching tender scene at the end of the movie on the end of the old West Pier before it was completely destroyed by fire, that moistens the eyes and pricks the heart.

The Fruit Machine is a beautiful slice and snapshot of life in 1980's England especially indicating the stark divide from the hard trodden unemployment core of Liverpool to the fanciful bright lights of seaside affluence in Brighton. It had much to say of society at the time and for a generation of disaffected gay youth harassed and discriminated against by the Conservative government of the time. It may have had farfetched and over extenuated scenes at times, but not only did it offer the gay youth a glimmer of hope in a grey and often persecuted real world, it was both real and apparitional escapism. There are a few moments where the film seems to flag or go slow, which caught the attention and the wrath of the critics, however get passed those and you have a wonderful example of 80's filmmaking.

"A wonderful and romantic romp through 1988, it is like a stroll down memory lane for those of us that came out in the late 80's. Where we really did have to knock on gay club doors to gain entry and even in some cases offer up a password or code before we could enjoy the delights of mirror balls, red velvet seats and Stock Aitkin & Waterman tracks. The Fruit Machine was way more than just a classic coming of age movie, it was an open window into a world of colour for closet teenage boys like me. It had romance in spades, the bond between the two boys spoke volumes, it was also camp, Robbie Coltrane in a yellow checked dress for example. It was a film of and for it's time and without a big Hollywood budget, you couldn't want for or expect more"

Peter, Brighton.

44

Head On

Director: Ana Kokkinos.

Starring: Alex Dimitriades, Pail Capsis, Julian Garner.

This bold film concentrates on a 24-hour period in the confused muddled world of Ari an engaging nineteen-year-old. He comes from a traditionally Greek background and is having a hard job coming to terms with both his Greek background in an Australia that does not much care for its immigrant population and his own sexuality. Ari, as most guy's his age are is obsessed with sex, he is a bit of a player, having a few rampant sexual encounters during the span of this film, whilst most are gay, he does not limit himself to the male sex, half-heartedly having a sexual liaison with the sister of one of his friends.

Ana Kokkinos the director is of Greek-Aussie descent, which automatically gives this tale an authentic guiding hand and some of the lines spoken by fictional characters are not that far removed from the reality of experience. This is a surprisingly gritty film, heavy on the hopeless dissatisfaction of life as a son or daughter of immigrants in a country that is no stranger to racial and economic tensions. Ari is a handsome boy; he has that rough, cheeky, yet handsomely provocative look that can melt hearts at one hundred paces. He uses those looks, along with his aggressive sexual hunger and heat to have random sex with older guys in dark alleyways, grabbing a quick fix before going back to hang with his equally dissatisfied mates. There isn't a clear road ahead for him, he knows that, yet could he be dreaming of a better tomorrow, the way most trouble teens do? It does not look like judging by a lot of the scenes and muddled moments.

He lashes out at his parents for their traditional conservative sentiments and ideals, he wants to live in a different way, he is rebelling against them as well as the Greek immigrant society that both protects and taunts him. He's caught in a no man's land of his own and societies making, he deliberately keeps a distance from two of his friends who are more open and out with their sexual identities, showing that Ari isn't exactly the most likeable of people, yet, at just nineteen he knows what it takes a lot of us a lifetime to realise – "I'm not going to make a difference, I'm not going to change a thing." It may be harsh, it may be frank, but it is true and even though you want him to make a real difference, you will have no doubt he will not! Head on is dark reality on film and as such is a little unsettling at times to view, although you've got to admire the incredible talent of Alex Dimitriades, who has gone on to be a celebrated actor in Australia. The film had nine nominations from the Australian film institute and received much acclaim from critics both in Australia and around the world for its harsh realities, passionate performances and authentic script.

"I never thought I'd see a character from my back ground shown on the TV or movie screen, I especially thought I'd never see a GAY character from my background shown on the TV or movie screen, but that is exactly what I saw in Head On. As an Australian Greek, I sort of thought we were invisible, until Head On showed Australia and the world that we were here, that we did exist." **Al, Sydney.**

"It is gruff and rough and hard to watch but so is life" Gregory, **St Louis.**

"Alex Dimitrades is a fine actor, wonderful taking us on a dark ride, his character in Head-on is nasty, dirty and on a downward spiral yet he's also likable. He lights up the screen from start to finish, no matter how graphic or how dark the action. Head On is a realistic story of coming of age in a difficult society at a different time. " **Harry, Melbourne.**

43

Zero Patience

Director: John Greyson.

Starring: John Robinson, Michael Callen, Von Flores, Dianne Heatherington.

I so wish I had a glass or two of whatever they were drinking when they thought up the idea of Zero Patience, I mean, hey now, a happy gay musical about how HIV started, with talking arseholes, ghost conversations, no illness, lie about who does and doesn't support AIDS research, alienate most people add dance numbers, songs, oh and don't forget bringing back to life a Victorian adventure pretending he's 170 years old and if people don't like it, pretend it's a satirical parody!

Some say this fearless musical wants to tell us the fictional story of the first ever AIDS patient is the best thing since the round wheel. Others hold a different opinion, claiming it did much more harm to social understanding to an already misunderstood disease. It takes a brave sort of creative person to want to take on a subject like AIDS and make a musical about the inaccuracies of some suggestions of how one person might have started and spread the pandemic disease that had already caused such misery to millions. That brave person was John Greyson a Canadian filmmaker who had started working on this project in the mid-eighties. The film was hard to finance and came out in 1993/94 thanks in part to UK's Channel 4.

Many of the issues and misconceptions regarding the disease were played out through songs, humour and parody, which had the film been released before the end of the eighties would have made some real and good impact. However, by the time it came out, society's knowledge of HIV/AIDS had improved dramatically. It certainly had some witty and amusing songs presented in a theatrical and vibrant way. I thought some parts were amusing, some vaguely interesting, yet because of various aspects and constraints it failed to live up to the promise and the audience deserved more that it got, however that notwithstanding, it still holds an influential place in gay cinema history.

"Zero Patience, was a remarkable film, it really took an anti-establishment view of AIDS introduction, well nearly, it made a joke of research that had

already been proved wrong that it was a monkey loving flight attendant that had caught the illness and spread it around the world while he was working. It is part drama, part musical, part comedy, part public information film, part puppet show and part historical re-enactment. It was fun, colourful, had some sexy guys in it." **Dave, Margate.**

"It's a low budget movie, awful acting, terrible singing, over the top production style, it seemed to be designed for the gay community, yet we already knew more accurate information about AIDs, preaching to the converted is a phrase that come to mind. If it hadn't have been made so gay then more straight people would have seen it, watched it all and then done some good. I think a lot of straight people didn't sit through it all and missed the point it was trying to make, that the whole zero patient idea was false and they came away believing it was true. But at least it had a go" **Anon**

"A vibrant and entertaining song-filled satire." **Jason King, Film Critic, Sydney.**

42

Taxi Zum Klo

Director: Frank Ripploh.

Starring: Frank Ripploh, Bernd Broaderup, Orpha Termin.

A film from the seventies, released in 1980, Taxi Zum Klo tells the story of a life divided by society and standards into two different parts, respectability by day and licentious indecency by night.

An autobiographic account from Frank Ripploh who by day was the respectable and liked schoolteacher yet by night a hedonistic, sex seeking, public toilet inhabiting cruiser. The bulk of the story is taken with Frank's need and desire to hunt for the latest sexual conquest and encounters in risky and unsavoury places. He meets and falls for a theatre manager and they move in together, could this be the end of his hunting for sex in the underbelly of the very edge of Berlin society? Another question raises itself, does he manage to keep his seedy sex life out of the classroom, even if he does from time to time he has been known to mark students work in the public lavatories he inhabits hunting for his next slice of cock?

This is a stark tale of promiscuity and the hedonistic freedom of the pre-AIDS days seemed to afford for certain members of our society. As this is, an autobiographical or semi-autobiographical tale it has an authentic quality to that is a fine mix between parody, caricature, honesty and realism. There is such sincerity in some scenes that have you anxious and worried for Frank and his vibrant lifestyle. It is a wonderful spotlight on the Berlin sexual subculture of the seventies as well as taking things to the absolute limit there are some lighter, tender and caring moments. The action has been spliced with snippets of old film including some of an erotic nature, yes I do really mean porn there, which only add to the quality and controversy of this picture.

As Ray, one of the blogging respondent's kindly pointed out, Taxi Zum Klo was originally refused a certificate and therefore could not be shown in cinemas on general release in the UK. They had to adopt a private club status in order to show the highly erotic film. Something that only a few were committed to doing so and thus a wide audience was denied the chance to experience Frank's wild side. There was, I am told, some form of edited VHS version of the film in circulation during the mid-eighties. It was feared the unedited version would be lost, however Film4 came to the rescue a few years ago, managed to get it passed by the BBFC and it was shown on late night television in its entirety. An uncut DVD was also available from Peccadillo Pictures.

"A film which is hardly ever mentioned these days yet was an absolutely seminal gay film when it came out.'Taxi Zum Klo', which appeared only a very short time before a certain AIDS appeared and brought so many lives crashing down.

When 'Taxi Zum Klo' was released in 1981 it was not allowed to be shown in public cinemas and my local picture-house (then in Oxford) had to convert itself into a private club for one week only in order to show the film. To get in you also had to purchase your membership of this club in advance, which I did, and I knew immediately that it was a film of some significance, covering, for one thing, the rampant promiscuity of the main Frank Ripploh character - though none of us knew then what was just around the corner.

A further curiosity about it was that, thanks to the then 'Child Protection Act', which came about largely because of pressure from one Mrs Mary Whitehouse and her ilk, there is a scene in the film which for British screens (even private ones) had to be blacked out, showing an old, short, scratchy piece of German film in which a man takes the hand of a young boy and puts it inside his fly. The bizarre thing about this was that this particular piece of film was compulsory viewing for children in German schools, highlighting the dangers of trusting strangers."

Ray, Worthing.

41

Trick
Director: **Jim Fall**

Starring: **Christian Campbell, John Paul Pitoc, Tori Spelling.**

A funny and amusing low budget movie that had a big impact, Trick is a jolly little story of two guys trying to get it on in the big city. It does not pretend to be anything more than it is a lightweight ineffective comic tale of finding a place to shag in New York City. It was made for an astonishing $450,000 and made a clear shed load over $2 million and almost as much in DVD sales and was shot in just over a week, now that's a good return if you ask me.

The stories goes a little like this; Gabriel a wannabe songwriter with writers block looks for stimulation and inspiration in some unusual places, one of which happens to be a sex club. In this raunchy venue that he see's handsome go-go boy Mark, played by the sexy scrummy honey John Paul Pitoc, yet has no way of meeting the young gentlemen of great cheekbones and perky pec's. However, you will never guess whom just happened to be on the subway sitting opposite him on the way home……yep Mr Go-Go Boy!

They talk, they chat and they want to do oh so much more than just chat, but where are they going to go to consummate their relationship. The whole film then revolves around the continued thwarting of their attempts to get on down to the rumpy pumpy hide the sausage sort of intimacy that all wannabe songwriters wish to do with go-go dancer boys. Trick has some jolly funny moments and some vaguely serious moments along the ride of their lives, but it is not supposed to be more than just a bit of a fun way to spend an hour and half. On paper, it should have flopped, by description it should have disappeared down the dumpster of

27

drama, but in reality, it was a smiley happy film that gave people a good time. No hidden messages, no serious meanings, just good fun escapist entertainment with a pretty cast and a lovely musical score. The influence it exerts is not perhaps overtly obvious, yet look at virtually all listings of the top fifty greatest, most enjoyable, most whatever and whatnot gay films complied in the last ten years and there is a ninety-eight per cent chance Trick will be mentioned somewhere in the mid or upper middle regions of that list. It may have been lightweight, it may have had a few flaws, but people liked it, remember it and suggest it and it remains in the top 100 most successful gay themed films of all time.

40

Boy Culture.
Director: Q. Allan Brocka.

Starring: Patrick Bauchau, Derek Magyar, Darryl Stephens, Jonathon Trent, George Jonson.

Boy Culture is Q. Allan Brocka's film adaptation of Matthew Rettenmund's critically acclaimed and remarkably expressive novel, it was first shown at the 2006 London Lesbian and Gay Film Festival. Mixed reactions from film critics around the gay world greeted it, 'well-packaged bit of overly familiar fluff' "sharper than the typical gay indie flick' 'the best gay themed movie since Mysterious Skin' 'Tired, dull, overacted, over directed waste of time' are just four examples. Yet continually, Boy Culture finds its way to a mid-point position on lists and compilations of best gay films of the last decade.

Boy Culture takes us on a nurturing tale of tangled relationships, mental, physical and emotional longing that requires maturing in a gay world that revolves around and is often over obsessed with youth. Edges of intergenerational relations, sexual ambivalence, expression, longing, deception and a recreated family dynamic box in this story of social marginalization and love.

This film centralises around the world of a well turned out male hooker on the higher end of the renting scale, you know the sort, no need for ads in the back of glossy free mags, word of mouth suffices. As befits a working boy of this standard, he keeps a working clientele rota of twelve regulars, which judging by his apartment and lifestyle, seem to pay him reasonably well for those intimate services rendered.

He adopts the name X, it is like a persona he wears for business purposes, only it is not just an pseudonym to hide behind at work, he uses it at home too. Home happens to be a fancy Seattle apartment which he shares with two others guys, a sexy black guy and fruity young scene queen twink boy. X is no 'heart of gold' whore, nor is he the tortured drug addicted man slag taking it up the chocolate starfish to fund his next fix. He is remarkably well rounded and mature, round and mature if you do not count the fact that he is emotionally retracted that is. He keeps his feelings well hidden from everyone, including himself most of the time. Classic example of this is the early revelation that he has not sex for pleasure since he was twelve years old, sex for business yes, regularly, weekly, but for pleasure, nope not a bit of it.

He secretly has a bit of a thing for one of his roommates, Andrew, the sexy black dude with a smouldering face and a body to die for, or die to be under, perhaps. He arrived from Portland some time ago after breaking off a relationship with the sister of a guy he desired most strongly. He is not one for the casual sex that seems to prevail around every single gay scene the world over, which to X makes him even more desirable.

Not following Andrew's example is the third inhabitant of this little cosmos, a campy late teen twink boy Joey who is rather loose with his virtue, exploring the gay scene with the vim and vigour that only one can when the candles on your birthday cake would not light up a small city! One of the key things about Joey you should also know at this stage, not that he's a little cutie, which he is, but that he has the hot's for and is secretly in lust / love with X.

So this little trio of maleness has eyes for each other in a somewhat muddled form, Andrew wants X, Joey wants X, X wants Andrew but who will get whom? You know it should be Andrew and X but they don't acknowledge or act on their feelings, it's enough to make you want to bang their heads together!

Following the death or something like that, of one if his clients, X has a vacancy among his twelve apostles, which is filled at surprising speed by an intriguingly grizzled mature man called Gregory, whom we learn hasn't left his apartment for eight years. The majority of the time that X spends with Gregory is spent talking, learning and listening. Stories of long ago, of love found and love ultimately lost from Gregory's side and tales of Andrew and Joey from X. Sex is not part of their usual routine, nope; you could be forgiven for forgetting X is actually a hooker by these scenes. They are actually quite a beautiful collection of cinematic treasures, relying heavily on spoken nuances of the communication and non-verbal cinematic visions. A story is, quite often told with just subtle eye movements and word inflections. It also helps that playing Gregory is the legendary Patrick Bauchau, whose voice and accent is so captivating and soul enhancing.

Andrew pleads with X to come with him to his ex's wedding, which he attends despite reservations, he pretends to be Andrews lover, at Andrews request, but it all turns rather confused and awkward and darn near farcical if it were not quite so touching.

The crux of this trip and after a visit to Gregory is a completely big reassessment of his life and his loves for dear old X, our hero. There is a clear almost 'OMG' moment of clarity and understanding when he finally comes to the conclusion that he cannot carry on be as emotionally aloof as a lone desert cactus. There will continue to be no meaning in his life until he can chip away his emotional straitjacket and open his eyes and heart to relationships.

Thus born is a happy and surrogate family, the three fine roommates find love in each other's arms, well sort of and it's a happy ever after ending. Sure, I've really curtailed that and snipped off a few plot shoots and the bedding plants just for brevities sake and to ensure you'll go out and watch it to find out what and who are the three, if love can survive, is there life after thirty in the gay world?

Boy Culture is as much about maturing relationships as it is about the life of a male hustler, the focus is how we all often evolve, how love may seem like one thing at first, but when examined further is something quite different and ultimately far more rewarding. There are some heavily placed scenes to include issues, to be a little confrontational, like the wedding scene in which black Andrew enters with white X hand in hand and nobody seems to notice either the handholding or the colour difference. We know we are all supposed to say, wow, is not that cool, isn't that special, and how sweet it is that mom pops a condom on the bed for them. It would be cool; it would be sweet, if it were not just a little bit too forced and jammed into the surrounding scenes. However, that said, it does not spoil the film, it enhances the general feeling of this amusing movie with a fine ensemble cast. It may not be the greatest films in the world, but it sure offers a lot of kooky good lines, soft passions and honestly. It doesn't matter what age you are you can always learn from those of another generation – above and below. Also, as we tread this promenade called life if you remain true to your feelings and you can't go much wrong, well you can, but you'll have nobody to blame other than yourself, and it's so much harder kicking your own arse!

"Boy Culture is a rare piece of gay movie making that doesn't seek to make you feel worthy of watching, it simply seeks to entertain, with a slightly pure look at the oldest profession of the all-time. It is a highly engrossing movie about the fragility of relations between friends and between generations. It is very provocative and evocative." **Ricky, Florida.**

39

Krampack

Director: Cesc Gay

Starring: Fernando Ramallo, Jordi Vilches.

Krampack is the original Spanish/European title of the film that was also known as Nico and Dani, and is a well thought out and slightly disturbing coming of age story on a sleepy Spanish costa. Krampack focuses on the antics of two engaging and appealing sixteen year-olds, who, thanks to wealthy parents seem to have a whole and rather posh beach house pretty much to themselves for a few weeks over summer.

Dani is the soft sensitive, slightly introspective dreamer who wants to be a writer, whilst Nico, the dark one is far more pragmatically fun loving and fast on his wits. The two teen lads are best friends, they are very close, so close in fact they might from time to time krampack with each other! Krampack is their word for a little indulgence in mutual masturbation, something that is commonplace between curious open and expressive continental teens.

This is essentially a tale of coming to terms with sexuality, one with his gayness and the other with his straightness and the way in which adolescent friendships change with the on-going burgeoning sexuality and maturity. Great performances from the young cast as they struggle from innocents to experienced, with a few little surprises along the way, not least an older and seemingly predatory gay writer. However, It's not all chocolates, hearts and flowers, there are some darker and oddly cruel harsh moments in what otherwise could have been just your usual rite of passage movie, these make it compelling viewing, especially among the teen and twenty-something Europeans

"There is a special place in my heart for Krampack, it helped me come to terms with my sexuality and understand things a lot better. It really is about growing up and finding your own way, difficult as that can be a times. It really is a gay movie too, Cese Gay!" **Nic, Switzerland.**

"It is so far removed from the traditional American style coming of age movies, giving it a purly European slant, which makes it refreshing and so much more honest. The scenery is beautiful, the acting superb and the way it delicately deals with emotion is amazing. All in all it is a wonderful film, about discoveries." **Benjamin, Oslo.**

38

Westler

Director: Wieland Speckt.

Starring: Siguard Rachman, Andy Lucas, Rainer Strecker.

Westler is a remarkably engaging mid-eighties film made for German television, which at its heart is a beautiful gay love story, but a love story with a difference.

Felix is a kindly amusing gay guy living in free West Berlin, a friend from America comes for a visit and together they cross the diving wall and enter East Berlin for a tourist day trip. Whilst over there they met a young East Berliner, Thomas. Thomas is intriguing, warming and slightly vulnerable; Felix instantly falls head over heels for him. Yet this is a love affair that will not run smoothing, there is a vast physical, political and social divide standing tall between them. Can they manage to maintain a relationship with such seemingly insurmountable obstacles in their way? Can love conquer all or is the Berlin wall to much of a mental as well as physical barrier?

Felix makes as many trips as possible to Thomas but it is these frequent trips that arise suspicions within the minds of the border guards. Things cannot stay the way they are and these appealing young gentlemen are forced into planning a dangerous escape to secure a more stable future together.

Westler is an interesting movie and a rare inside look at life either side of the wall that divided a city for so long. A lot of the East Berlin footage was clandestinely filmed on that side of the border in 1984/85 and the differences are startling. The film stands as a testament of the harsh sparse prison-like conditions endured by the inhabitants of East Berlin under communist rule. It is also a wonderfully expressive love story of divided difficulties, which is heart-warming and passionate.

"Probably the best German gay movie ever made, passionately filmed and acted depicted love between two people that lived only three kilometres from each other, yet lived in different worlds. They manage to make relationship work despite the great hardships enforced upon them. Homosexuality was still a taboo subject when this was made in East Berlin further increasing

difficulties for these two boys. The border guards from memory were more aggressive than depicted here but maybe my memory is at fault. Enjoyable, entertainment and historical value in Westler is abundant and recommend."
HS, Berlin.

37

Caravaggio

Director: Derek Jarman

Srarring: Nigel Terry, Sean Bean, Tilda Swinton, Dexter Fletcher.

Caravaggio the funky heavily stylised fictionalisation, readdressed life story of the artist formerly known as Michelangelo Merisi da Caravaggio.

Oh yes, if you want an 'arty' film then this one is for you, a wonderful and imaginative retelling of the life of Caravaggio through the inspirational eyes of Derek Jarman, who takes some unexpected turns in creating this cinematic treasure.

Ultimately, this is a story of Caravaggio life, told in an episodic film segment style, opening with the painter popping off this realm from lead poisoning in exile, his only companion being Jerusaleme, a supposedly deaf and dumb muse. Incidentally, the parents gave Jerusaleme, to Caravaggio when he was just a small boy.

Caravaggio then dreams back, or replays his life, first as a bit of a teenage streetwise hood ducking and diving, hustling a bit here and there while he paints. That's pictures not wall, but I guess you knew that already! The oddly handsome and entirely open Dexter Fletcher who adds a certain innocent charm yet knowing eye to the role of the character of the young Caravaggio. The young artist is taken ill and is cared for by priests, never a fully good thing in my book and it is whilst he's being cared for, he pulls in the attention of Cardinal Del Monte. The cardinal sees a future for the teenager, thus nurtures the boy's artistic leanings and intellectual development oh and he also has a bit of a fumble with the fresh face and nubile young skin.

Back as an adult Caravaggio remains funded and lives under Del Monte's roof and takes input from the cardinal. However, he also takes in street people, whores and drunks to play models for his art, which are usually vibrant, aggressive religious paintings and creations. During this portion of film and Caravaggio's life, he is showing as a hedonistic man, drinking heavily, gambling, fighting and fornicating with both male and female lovers.

Ranuccio is a bare-knuckle street fighter with an interesting face, played by the talented Sean Bean, the allure of the masculine Ranuccio is not lost on

Caravaggio, who eyes the rough fighter as perhaps model or maybe a lover, although it is most probably both. During one of these sessions, Ranuccio's introduces Caravaggio to Lena, his girlfriend, acted by the striking Tilda Swinton. Rather confusingly she also becomes an object of attraction to the artist, in both the model and lover capacities. Separately, Ranuccio and Lena are caught kissing Caravaggio, displaying jealousy over the artist's attentions, it's amusing and one can only wonder what is the motivation, money, affection or being immortalised in art?

Oh shock, horror and hells bells, Lena announces she's pregnant and although she doesn't say who the father is, she, says she's going to become the live in mistress to Scipione Borghese, a rich merchant of some sort. Things are not quite, as they seem, before the month is gone, she is found murdered. Caravaggio and Jerusaleme clean Lena's body whilst Ranuccio looks on and we see Caravaggio painting her and seemingly wriggles around erotically with her naked dead body.

Ranuccio is arrested for Lena's murder, however Caravaggio pops off to see the Pope and the fighter is released. You see it pays to have friends in high places, or at least know where their dirty laundry is kept. Ranuccio who had previously protested his innocence loudly calmly informs Caravaggio he actually did kill Lena, so they could be together. Oh, life is so confusing, so muddling and so utterly Roman, Caravaggio far from being happy at this declaration of love slits Ranuccio's throat. The ending of the movie sees Caravaggio on his deathbed, flicking between visions of himself and refusing the last rites.

It is heavy on the homoeroticism and sexual intrigue; it combines accurate period drama with fantasy, fiction and many inconsistences. Some like the little odd touches, such as watches, calculators, vans, electric lights as an homage to Caravaggio's style, others see them as sloppy filmmaking errors or pointless attempts to anchor the historic story in modern times. I personally make no comment on that area, all I will say is that Caravaggio is a wonderful example of Jarman's work, creative, colourful, interestingly different and not without its own controversies.

Influential, well The Washington Post called it 'An act of Vandalism' self-indulgent was another barb fired at it by various critics, guaranteeing it an impact and an audience. It along with other Jarman works have gone down in history as instrumental in the development of the UK's gay cinema industry.

36

Prayers for Bobby

Director: Russell Mulcahy.

Starring: Sigourney Weaver, Ryan Kelley, Henry Czemy.

A made for TV movie, Prayers For Bobby was first broadcast on American TV over the weekend of 24th/25th January 2009 amassing an audience of 6.1 million people. It tells the true story of Mary Griffith, whose teenage son, Bobby, committed suicide due to her religious intolerance to his sexuality, forcing her to re-evaluate her religious views and her life.

Sigourney Weaver takes on the lead role of Mary Griffith in this emotive and powerful made for TV movie, for which she has received a number of awards and nominations. Mary is a devout Christian and believes in the ultra-conservative teachings of the Presbyterian Church; of course, she raises her children that way. All is well, until one of sons, Bobby confesses to his brother that he might be gay and that is the day the whole family's lives changed forever.

All in Bobby's immediate family start to come to terms with his homosexuality, except his mother, oh no, she believes in the power of god, she believes god can cure her son of the illness that is afflicting him. She makes him pray harder, do church chores, she takes him to a psychiatrist, she does not let up and Bobby, well really wants his mother's approval, he wants to make her happy, so he tries his best. The churches dim view on homosexuality, his mother's overbearing attempts to control his behaviour leave Bobby depressed, withdrawn and on edge.

He moves to Oregon, staying with a cousin, hoping one day his mother will accept him for who and what he is, yet feel incredibly guilty for not being able to overcome his homosexuality for her sake. Whilst there he meets David in a gay bar and they start a relationship. Mary, his mother does not want him to continue the way he is, Bobby knows this, and he feels it deeply in his heart. He wishes he could be a better son, the perfect son, but he knows he will never be that boy in his mother's eyes. One night as his depression plunges new depths, he allows himself to fall from a highway bridge right into the path of one of those massive trucks. He is killed instantly and the Griffith family are given the devastatingly horrific news the very next day. During the next part of the film we see Bobby's mother, Mary question her own behaviour, her beliefs and the views of the church regarding homosexuality. It is a deeply emotional, personal and enlightening journey. It tells the story of how Mary Griffith became a gay rights activist, how she spoke out with a simple message against all forms of homophobia and continues to speak out.

Prayers for Bobby deals well with the Christian fundamentalism that conditions Mary Griffith to believe her son would burn in hell for all eternity such is the immensity of the evil of homosexuality. There are some strange aspects in the dialogue, but also good salient points made, thanks in part to the real Bobby, for he penned a series of journals, which ensured his side of the story was told, giving the young man a voice in death that he never attained in life.

American made for TV movies don't usually have a great reputation for stunning acting, however Prayers For Bobby is the exception to that rule, Weaver is absolutely superb as Mary, both before Bobby's suicide and after. You really feel her pain and agony as she comes to terms with her part in her son's death, a monumental moment for any parent. Bobby is played by Ryan Kelley who does extremely well with gut wrenching emotion and honesty. Sure, this is not a perfect movie, it has a few flaws like the regular fade to a black out where the ads would go on telly, but it is a wonderful expressive story told remarkably well. It will make your eyes moist.

"You have to have Prayers For Bobby in your list, it is a bloody amazing movie, Sigourney Weaver is amazing playing a really right wing Christian mother who goes to great efforts to rid her son of gayness. It aint just 'pray the gay way' its everything. It is so sad that its one her son jumping off that highway bridge that makes her start to see that conversion aint possible and its aint so bad being gay. It is so powerful that you long for a happy ending, which you know aint gonna happen." **Bob, Fort Lauderdale.**

"Prayers For Bobby should be shown in churches all over the world that condemn gay people in such a way it causes real harm. Its time to stop the pain" **Tara, Missouri.**

35

The Laramie Project.

Director: **Moises Kaufman.**

Starring: **Christina Ricci, Laura Linney, Peter Fonda, Joshua Jackson.**

The Laramie Project is a dramatic and heartbreakingly commanding film premiered at the 2002 Sundance Film Festival and broadcast on American television network HBO in March of that year.

Matthew Shepard, was born in December 1976, he was a political science student at Wyoming university in a town called Laramie, he was an approachable young man with a passion for equality and stood firm for acceptance of peoples differences, yet it wasn't through his life his name because known the world over, it was his death. It was shortly after midnight on 6th October 1996 that Matt bumped into Aaron McKinney and Russell Henderson at the Fireside lounge. Nobody can be sure why Matt chose to go off with these two men; however, they drove him to an isolated rural area where they viciously, violently beat and tortured him. They battered him, robbed him and tied him to a fence where they just left him there to die. For eighteen hours, slight Matt Shepard remained tied to the fence, hovering in and out of consciousness before slipping into a coma. The next day, a cyclist who first thought the ghoulish sight tied to the fence was not a human but a scarecrow put up early for Halloween, found him. Matt had two significant and sizable skull fractures, one at the back and one in front of his right ear, which caused severe brain and brain steam damage. There were over a dozen lacerations to his neck, face and head, he was so brutally beaten about head that his face was covered and caked in his own blood. The only part of his face not coated in his blood were his cheeks, where the tracks of his tears had washed away the blood. Matt Shepard did not regain consciousness and died just before one am on 12th October 1998.

Matthew Shepard was murdered purely because of his homosexuality, news of his horrific murder sent shockwaves of outrage and revulsion throughout the local community, America and the world.

The Laramie Project is not a biographical story of Matt's life, it is not a dramatization of his death, nor is it an psychological investigation into the minds of his killers or their subsequent trial. No, The Laramie Project is a deeply moving exploration of the effect Matt's murder had on the town's people of Laramie.

It was based on the play of the same name, which saw members of a small theatre company go to Laramie in the weeks and months after Matt's murder, interviewing and speaking with the real inhabitants of Laramie. It is from these interviews, those accounts, combined with journals and news reports that the play and film was created, showing the real reaction to Matt's beating and death. The majority of dialogue employed during the film are the actual spoken words of those real residents.

Together the play and movie were written and directed by Moisés Kaufman and he employs a typical yet gripping documentary style here, cutting between actors portraying local residents and real news reports of the crime, as well as a few dramatic recreations, there is political commentary and even real trial transcripts. The Laramie Project is not some slick Hollywood flick or some glossy dramatization of events that did not happen; this is a cinematic spotlight on the real reactions, the real horror of a violent and tragic end because of prejudice and hate.

Whilst it may at times be harrowing and hard to watch, how a tale of a young man being savagely beaten and left for dead, not be, yet it is no less an important and exceptionally emotional experience. As a gay man, the news of Matthew Shepard's death and each subsequent death of other gay people, abused, murdered, bullied because of their sexuality feels like a hammering punch to the gut, each is painful, which makes The Laramie Project achingly emotive, but it is equally empowering, good things come from watching this movie.

The cast list is impressive; especially considering they only received nominal payment for their time, some received nothing other than travelling expenses. The impetus and drama never lulls, the emotion is always intense, although what else would you, or could you expect from a film of this type, genre and background? It is vastly different from the play, being a third shorter and played by way more than the eight actors that take to the stage; it loses none of the important ingredients that make this story work. This is not a perfect film, but you do not have to have perfection to have a great example of how influential motion pictures can or indeed, should be. My thoughts are this should be made compulsory viewing in secondary and high schools around the world, accepting our differences is the key to not only our happiness, but our very survival. The Laramie Project will continue to be an influential and important movie as well as social document for as long as crimes of hate and discrimination like this continue.

"I don't know how influential you think it was, but I suggest The Laramie Project, moved me to tears, it still moves me to tears" **Alexander, Paris.**

"Not sure a made for telle movie really counts in your criteriour, but may I suggest Laramie Project, about Matthew Shepards death. It is so moving and so powerful because it is the real reactions of what happened after he was attacked. It is well acted, nicely put together and so very moving." **Steve, Blogworld.**

"It's heart wrenching, touching, with gritty realism and honesty as you hear views, beliefs and statements from those really there. Yes there are some 'dramatic' moments, and rather than being completely one sided, as it so easily could have been, it's not, it includes hateful people with view that easily disgust, but, this gives the true picture of what really happened." **Jason King, Film Critic, Sydney.**

34

A.K.A.

Director: Duncan Roy.

Starring: Matt Leitch, Diana Quick, Lindsey Coulson, George Asprey, Bill Nighy.

A.K.A. is not about the Australian Karting Association, nor is it a flick about kickboxing in America and please don't get it confused with the sorority of Alpha Kappa Alpha or you will have some very angry sisters on your tail! A.K.A the film has been described as a modern-day Pygmalion, an interesting and sometimes a mesmerising study and expose of the British class system at is disaffected best, or should that be worst?

Dean is your average shy, working-class lad from Romford, he's been kicked out of home by his rather abusive stepfather. As all essentially good, yet slightly rough Essex kids down on their luck, he heads for the big city, yep London town. Oh yes, there are movie traditions at play here, but then again, this story is based on the real life, or very nearly, adventures of writer and director Duncan Roy. Somehow in the big bad capital city good things arrive for Duncan, opps I mean Dean and he manages to hook up with socialite gallery owning art dealing Lady Gryffoyn, a perfectly cast Diana Quick. He luxuriates in the wealthy life of champagne, aristocracy, cocaine, boys of the night all provided willingly and wantonly by the Lady Gryffoyn.

All goes swimmingly well, Dean loves the excesses of it all, until Lady Gryffoyn's son, Alexander, comes home for the holidays and does not take too kindly to Dean's presence in his mother's house and affections. It is a little messy, a little stagey and the long and short of it are that Dean up's and offs. He takes a hike and ends up in Paris, where he lives not on his wits, but the stolen credit card of Alexander, passing himself off as the young toff, his new life is one of duplicity and deception. The high life continues all thanks to the money of Gryffoyn, but before too long the fraud squad is on his tail. Dean, pretending to be Alexander, is the toast of the upper crust gay society, wining, dining, and mixing everything up, not least of all his own identity. Sooner rather than later the authorities catch up with him and the whole deck of cards along with a dream or two are strewn all over the floor.

One of the most striking aspects of this intriguing little movie is the split three-screen dimension employed pretty much throughout the almost two hours. Three panels of vision appear on the screen, often different angles or views of the same action and scene. Other times you see different aspect or back stories in one or other of the panels on screen, which add an interesting element to the film, which once you get used to, is rather fun. If you are not sure, what I mean then try to think watching a bank of security monitors and you will not go far wrong. At times rather than watching a movie, it feels as if you are being a tad voyeuristic on the lives unfolding in the three hidden camera panels before your eyes. I'm not sure that is completely intentional although for me it was both interesting and slightly distracting, I felt more distanced and separate from the action that any sense of solidarity or feeling for the characters is virtually impossible. Attention therefor is required in full at all times, so no nipping away make a cupper for the cat or to put the boyfriend out.

There are some interesting sexual dynamics at play here which I would have liked to have been further explored and expanded upon, but I guess this is not a tale about my life; it is Roy's semi-fictionalised life story. More seems to be made of the divisions of class, which is vaguely interesting to watch, even if Roy employs the typical and conventional middle class view that the rich are idle, cruel, unkind, unfeeling one-dimensional and the poor working class are simple, under educated rough people with intuitive criminal behavioural traits and tendencies. It isn't for me to say how realistic and accurate these depictions of class in the late seventies are, however I will say, they do tend to grind before the end is in sight, but then stereotypes very often do.

Matthew Leitch seems a talented actor with his portrayal of Dean, being incredibly engaging, interesting to watch and rather canny with his looks and eye movements. Diana Quick the most outrageous snob in real life who plays pretty much the same role repeatedly does the same here, although it is done without feeling, it is still executed with professionalism as do the rest of the cast, even if there is a lacking of passion.

"AKA is an intelligent, thought provoking and beautifully directed drama which presents a perfect example of the social divisions in the British class system, a marvel." **Jason King, Film Critic, Sydney.**

"I had thought the British class system had long gone, or if not gone completely, of less importance and much more irrelevant to the lives of ordinary people. AKA told me a different story, as an outsider it was interesting to watch, seeing the different social classes go about there day to day lives. Fascinating to see for me, although I am not all convinced it is as correct as we are told it is. The gay undercurrent storyline is great, as are some of the erotic scenes, but I would have thought there would have been more to it, or at least going to some kind of conclusion. It seems it was just added in as an extra attempt to make the story more interesting." **Tig, Sweden.**

33

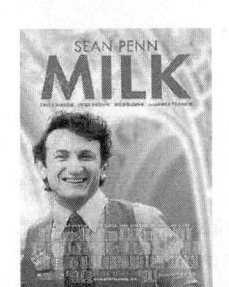

MILK

Director: Gus Van Sant

Starring: Sean Penn, Emile Hirsch, Josh Brolin, James Franco, Diego Luna.

Sean Penn stars in a career defining moment as Harvey Milk, a man synonymous with America's gay rights struggles of the seventies. Milk became the first openly gay elected official in the state of California and this incredibly compelling biopic chronicles the later stages of the gay rights activist as he rises through the political ranks to hold public office.

Milk The film was released to much acclaim in November of 2008 amassing a total box office take of around fifty-five million dollars, picking up four BAFTA and eight Academy award nominations along the way, winning two of the latter for best actor in a leading role and best original screenplay. It proved a big hit with the film critics, including even rather surprisingly those from the evangelical Christianity Today.

The film begins with real archive footage of police raids on America's gay bars, arresting and clubbing the clientele, which gives a gritty, realistic kick to the film, ensuring we know these were not happy and enlightened times to be living in as an openly gay male. An announcement details Milk's assassination follows, then we cut to Milk celebrating his 40th birthday in 1970, he was living in New York City at the time and had not yet made the move west to San Francisco. This is important because it shows his first meeting with the younger Scott Smith and chronicles the dissatisfaction they feel with life in the big apple.

It's all up sticks and like many gay men of their time, they move to America's west coast and San Francisco to be precise, hoping for a better way of life, more freedom, more acceptance of their sexuality and less prejudice.

They open a little camera shop on Castro Street called 'Castro Camera' in the heart of Eureka Valley, a working class neighbourhood in the process of evolving into a predominantly gay neighbourhood. During the production of the film, they actually took over Milk's old shop, now a gift boutique, to add a full authentic setting and base to the action. It is not all easy going as there is still opposition here, mainly from the old Irish-Catholics, however to this challenge, Milk rises and a gay activist is formed. For a bit at the start Scott

Smith works as Milk's campaign manager, but his frustration grows with Milk's devotion to politics, and the younger man makes his leave

An openly gay male running for office in 1970's America is not going to be an overnight success and there are two unsuccessful bids to become a city supervisor in 73 and 75, finally Milk wins a seat on the San Francisco Board of Supervisors in 1977 for District 5. It is this watershed victory, which makes him the first openly gay man to be voted into major public office in California. Milk meets fellow supervisor Dan White, a former police officer, fire fighter and Vietnam vet. White, a politically and social conservative has a very terse and challenging relationship with Milk, which leads to growing resentment. However, that said, they still evolve and a while later Milk attends the christening of White's first child. Dan White asks for Milk's assistance in preventing a psychiatric hospital from opening in White's district, possibly in exchange for White's support of Milk's citywide gay rights ordinance. However, Milk does not support White's opposition to the hospital for the negative effect it will have on troubled youth, which kicks White's resentment into high gear. He becomes the sole vote against the gay rights ordinance.

Milk launches a campaign to defeat Proposition 6, an initiative on the California state, which seeks to ban gays and lesbians and anyone who supports them, from working in California's public schools. This might seem preposterous in itself, but was part of a nationwide conservative movement that at the time sought to bar gay men from working in public schools or in public office. Thanks mainly to Milk and his team of supporters the bill is defeated on 7th November 1978, White is not happy, neither are several Christian right groups. White seems a little unstable and resigns from the board, only to ask for his place back a short time later. During the morning of 27th November, White sneaks his way into city hall, shoots George Moscone, the mayor in his office, and then goes to meet Milk, where he also shoots him, the fatal bullet delivered in execution style.

Sean Penn, whilst he may hold strong anti-British tendencies, beliefs and views, was incredible, passionate, resonant and believable as Harvey Milk, this is clearly a career best for him and a worthy Oscar win. He portrays Milk with a sense of class, passion and sensitivity from the very outset, which is both refreshing and surprising. Those in the know, tell me he nailed Harvey perfectly even to the point of accurately recreating his sing songish voice and trademark optimism. The film recaptures the political, religious and social intolerances of the times perfectly, yet sadly, was not unique to that period. At the time of its release, California was seeing the same level of intolerance and discrimination over the gay marriage proposition 8, a battle still not completely rectified.

The influence of this movie is sometimes masked by the disparaging mainstream media, the religious right, however, it reached much further than any other biopics about gay rights activists ever has before. It shone a bright and public light on to the life of a remarkable man who may have not been quite so well known outside of gay society. It highlighted a time of incredible discrimination and hatred, which surprised some in Middle America, yet refocused attention to the current fight against inequality, pushing it to the forefront of the public consciousness, which cannot be a bad thing at all.

32

To Wong Foo, Thanks For Everything Julie Newmar.

Director: Beeban Kidron

Starring: Wesley Snipes, John Leguizamo, Patrick Swayze, Stockard Channing, Jason London, Chris Penn, Blythe Howard.

A colourful drag queen road trip extravaganza of Hollywood does a Pricilla Queen of the Desert. It is a high power and high camp attempt to hijack the whole 'drag queens on a road trip' feel that was going on at the time. There was a lot of money thrown at this film, which shows in places, there was also a lot of speculation on whether it would be a success. Could it appeal to both gay and straight audiences, both young and old? Well, throw up a lot of money, hire three big Hollywood moviestars, mix in some crazy designers, some straight guys idea of high camp and straight girls ideas of what drag queens are all about and you've got To Wong Foo! Am I sounding harsh? Perhaps just a little, for it is a fine an upstanding movie and worthy of a mention in the hall of gay movie fame and that is mainly for not only putting Patrick Swayze in a dress, but for also making him a beauty contest winner!

On paper and just by the sound of it, this movie should have been a big flop, it should have bombed and somehow I am surprised it did not. There are stereotypes galore, there are scrip flaws, there is dodgy camera work, but overall, this headfirst dive into the pool of drag holds its own! The critics seemed to be fairly kind and the audience numbers quite impressive as were the DVD sales in what really is a pretty unrealistic expose life as a drag queen.

Noxeema Jackson, Vida Boheme, and Chi Chi Rodriguez are the queens of the show; they are in the mood to show America what it means to be a drag queen. The three top stars and winners of New York's drag queen beauty pageant decide to hit the road in a convertible. I am told it is a Cadillac but that means little to many of us Brits, yet they head off into the wilds to cross America heading for the bright lights of tinsel town. It is a drag queens on the road movie, so just what you would expect, the car breaks down and leaves our three queens of fabulous in a dusty small and incredibly dysfunctional mid-western town called Snydersville! Now, this isn't Blackpool, Brighton or San Francisco, drag queens are about as common in this part of America as snowmen are in the Sahara and much of the films charm and amusement is how the locals view and deal with these interlopers from what is, pretty much, another world.

There are flashes of glamour and bangs of glitter and the three queens of drag fab up the local town and the inhabitants, righting wrongs, ending feuds, broken hearts mended, giving the mute their voice and other such unbelievable items of goodness. Then once all the good work is completed, they leave small town America all the better for having had the camporee of flouncy fabric, glitter and sparkle and head on up to road to Hollywood for another drag queen contest and meet the legendary Julie Newmar.

This was a more popular choice among the heterosexual people I asked during the research of this project which I found rather interesting. It was also a lot more popular over the American side of the big pond that separates us, other than the stars and the location; I cannot quite see why that would be. Although for many this movie is seen as much more than a drag queen road trip sort of film and takes on many moral and ethical dilemmas, not least what colour lippy to wear with a red and blue chiffon number. There are hidden depths in how the three fake females are in some ways much more feminine than perhaps some, if not all the real women, but really, they are still men in dresses, this still extolling the power to hold their own against overbearing and controlling men.

It is an enjoyable film that is without doubt, although it only as deep as the foundation on their faces and as such incredibly lightweight compared to Pricilla, it still performs a wonderful function. It perhaps did more to open up homosexuality and female impersonation to Middle America than the aforementioned Queen of the Desert, but it did not have the same sparkle, glitz and sense of fun.

"I loved seeing Patrick Swayze in drag, need I say more?" **Dean, London.**

"Really it came too soon after Pricilla to really make much of an impact and perhaps for some there was just only so many drag queens travelling across a country you could take. However, watch it now and it's more enjoyable, even if it does follow the typical American method of always having morality in a movie." **Simon, Glasgow.**

31

Lilies

Director: John Greyson

Starring: Jason Cadieux, Matthew Ferguson, Danny Gilmore, Remy Girard, Brent Carver.

Lilies is captivating yet disturbing story in which a Catholic bishop is taken hostage in a Quebec prison in 1952 by his boyhood friend and prison inmate, terminally ill Simon. The bishop is there to hear the last confession of Simon, but unbeknown to him, Simon and his fellow prison inmates have very different intentions. They stage an elaborate, intricate and intimate recreation of the life shaping events of their youth some forty or so years previously.

Lilies is a 1996 Canadian film directed by John Greyson and is a faithful adaptation by Michel Marc Bouchard of his own play, Les feluettes with the help of Linda Gaboriau. The format and style are somewhat unorthodox yet intriguingly effective and thoughtfully presented a real play within a film. The action focuses around a recreation of historic events from the lives of the two central characters, Jean Bilodeau and Simon Doucet, in the prison chapel with inmates taking on the roles. This recreation is interceded with more full dramatizations or realist scenes, yet these are blended so well together, that they intimate the realist scenes are the imagination of the players. Elements of the realist or dramatized scenes are placed in the chapel to aid this effect, such as water and fallen leaves. In addition, even during the recreated dramatized realist scenes, the female characters are played by the male prison inmates, which adds a layer of believability to them, which would not have been possible with females taking the roles. It is a masterly touch that could have gone horrible wrong, spoiling a wonderful thought provoking story, yet it works perfectly and Lilies is so much the better for it.

During the film we follow local bishop, Jean Bilodeau, played with sanguine sincerity by Marcel Sabourin, the local bishop, he is delivered to the local prison under the auspices of hearing the last and final confessions of Simon Doucet, a dying inmate and former childhood friend, acted well by Aubert Pallascio. However once he takes his seat in the confessional, bishop Bilodeau is locked in and forced to confront the past bought to life by Doucet's fellow prisoners.

The scene playing out goes back to 1912, when Bilodeau and Doucet were childhood and school friends. It was a period in their young lives when they were experience things for the first time and coming to terms with feelings, emotions and sexual identity. Roberval seems like an idyllic place in which to spend ones childhood and adolescence, Simon starts has delicate and loving romantic relationship with Vallier, impeccably affected by the enchantingly good-looking Danny Gilmore.

The boy Bilodeau remains sexually repressed and tries desperately to convince Simon to join the seminary with him, believing their salvation lies within the confines of the church. Bilodeau, Vallier and Doucet are involved in a school play, which deals with dramatizing the martyrdom of Saint Sebastian, Simon taking the lead role. Undoubtedly, the homoerotic undertones of the Saint Sebastian play contribute to Bilodeau's sexual awakening and his burgeoning love for Simon.

However, Simon only has eyes for Vallier, such is the power of their love and attraction, Bilodeau recognizes the true nature of the relationship and confronts them both one afternoon immediately after play rehearsals. Simon and Vallier pacify Bilodeau in order that Simon can force an oddly passionate kiss upon him, perhaps offering a taste of what he will never get. Into the middle of this melee stumbles Vallier's mother, the Countess de Tilly, played with aplomb by Brent Carver, this forces Simon to halt the kiss and flee. Vallier's mother is a dreamer, preferring to mainly live within the memories of her former life, yet announces the arrival of an exotic aristocrat from Paris, arriving by hot air balloon.

The whole village is out for the arrival of this socialite of Parisian aristocracy, Vallier's mother somewhat unwittingly details the passionate kissing between the young Bilodeau and Doucet. Simon's father hears this and is none too pleased, he retreats home, beats the boys so violently the young lad needs medical attention for his wounds. It is whilst seeing a doctor he bumps into the young Parisian baroness. Now, because of his beating, he renounces his love for Vallier and pretends to fall in love with the baroness, even going as far as engagement.

Vallier's mother whilst may not be playing with a full deck upstairs, she can still see her beautiful son is smitten to the point of madness with Simon. She encourages him to head off to the engagement party and declare his love for Simon. He does and their love is reunited, as only it could and should be. The baroness, feelings all in tatters, spills the beans on the truth of Vallier's father; he is not coming back to her, living it up in Paris with a new wife and child.

Simon and Vallier have a wonderfully touching intimate and romantic encounter after the party, which is exquisitely crafted on dramatization and play. After which, Vallier's now completely unhinged mother says that she will be going to Paris, and invites Simon and Vallier to see her off. Instead, she takes them to the woods, where she plonks herself down into a shallow grave. She pleads for Vallier strangle her to death so she can avoid the shame, pity and derision holstered at her door. The deed is done and her body covered in an incredibly emotive moment. Such was the society of the day that reputation was everything and once that was gone, a person had little standing.

The boy Bilodeau witnesses the murder, is spurred to confess his love for Simon. When he is rejected, he sets ablaze the attic room where Vallier and Simon are staying and maliciously locks the two lovers inside.

There is no escape, no ventilation, the only way free is locked, death is inevitable, however Bilodeau is remorseful, he returns just in time to pull Simon to safety, yet not only does he leave Vallier in the room to burn. He also falsely informs the policemen arriving at the scene that Vallier is already dead and rescue futile.

The poignant end to the play reveals that it is Vallier's murder for which Simon Doucet had been arrested, convicted and now serves sentence for. Thus, this whole elaborate reincarnation of the past is to elicit final confession not from Simon, but from Bishop Bilodeau.

Lilies is an amazingly and achingly beautiful cinematic work of rather rare astonishing intelligence and magnificence. The cinematography is so expressive and cherished it defies space and time to afford a world of enchanting possibilities and far reaching depths without stretching reality to extremes. The script and characterisation are delicately balanced and spiced to perfection with the Shakespearean theme of forbidden love and humanities predispositions. There are many times during the unfolding action that you want to tell, shout, scream and implore with the actors over their choices, ideals or beliefs, such is the plausibility, credibility and emotional authenticity of the various parts of the movie. The luscious quality of the musical score should not go unmentioned, for it truly conveys the message and helps the action along with understated charm and love. The cast are exceptional, especially Jason Cadieux, Danny Gilmore and Matthew Ferguson and fully deserve the praise heaped upon them. Lilies was never a big hit with either the critics or at the box office, its limited release having major drawbacks, yet it seems to receive glowing reviews from all that have seen it, myself included. Exceptional cinema, emotively influential if not overly successful.

30

I Think I Do

Director: Brian Sloan

Starring: Alexis Arquette, Jamie Harrold, Christian Maelen, Lauren Velez, Tuc Watkins.

Take a pinch for Four weddings and a Funeral, a flick or two of The Boys in the Band, then slide in a whole slab of Friends, don't forget a gram or two of Partridge Family, shake it up, add the pink fairy dust of gaydom, bake for three weeks and a day and you've got yourself a gay film called 'I Think I Do'. A sparkling though rather corny movie drawing from tried and oh so wearily tested familiar social formula that drags more than just a little. It is supposed to be a delicately sweet comedy with a side serving of romance, yet a cutting script, one dimensional characters and dated soundtrack means it and therefore, you, never know quite exactly what it is, or trying to be. I am not saying it is a bad film, no far from it, bad it is not, but good? Well, that's up to you to decide, however when conducting research for this book, I Think I do was suggested a fair few times, interestingly enough only by people in their twenties. Therefore, it is obviously having an impact with a certain demographic of our rich, vibrant and colourful society. Yet, I believe this film didn't always warrant some of the bad press it seemed to receive around it's release - 'Badly acted, badly written and badly directed' San Francisco Chronicle, 'The whole thing is terribly condescending' Montreal Mirror, 'Nothing outstanding, no redeeming qualities' Rainbow Press. It may have been too soft to be the screwball comedy Brian Sloan may have desired and its limited original cinema release was a long way from breaking even, it still has something offer, if only lukewarm entertainment.

In brief, the central storyline revolves around two young guys, best friends, one of them gay and the other one straight. Bob is the gay one, played rather brightly by Alexis Arquette, and Brendan the straight one, played by Christian Maelen. One night during some drunken malarkey and high-jinks Bob misinterprets the situation and goes for a full on grope session of poor hettie Brenden and quite reasonably a rift forms between them.

That was years ago and now the former college roommates are reuniting for a mutual friends' wedding and things are very different now. Cute little Bob is now a successful scriptwriter of an American daytime TV soap who is dating the handsome, vain and dim leading actor under the stonkingly great porn name Sterling Scott. Brendan is a successful Teacher living the traditional straight guy life in a Boston suburb.

Things are not exactly what they seem and you know the straight boy is perhaps not so straight anymore and he has the fluttering heart for his former roomie. The relationship ebbs and flows over the bulk part of the film with some funny and interesting padding by a good surrounding cast, but you know the ending already. It is just the getting there that is going to be difficult, so the will he or won't he ethic becomes the when the flipping eck is he going to get it.

There is a jollity to these cinematic pictures that flash before your eyes with his light and easy to follow and wash over you like a wind from a hot air blower. You do not have to think too hard for this movie, which perhaps is why some have suggested it for influential, although for something that is supposed to be hard and screwball it is a little too simpering and sweet. Depth is not the key word here with this movie, but you know, do we always want to be deep and brooding?

"I Think I Do is a wonderful drama comedy about a group of friends from college who really are all in a tumble for love. It is pretty and the sexy cast make sure there is plenty to look at, but it is more about longing and wishing than what things look like on the surface. Reversing the tables, the gayboy wants to boff the sexy straight college jock, gets viciously and badly turned down. Only when they meet years later we find the sexy straight jock is not straight any longer and wants to boff the cute little gayboy, who goes to turn down the straight jock. I loved the way it turned out and that Scott Stirling character is hot!" **Adam, Southampton.**

"A vivacious and incredibly likeable film that had a huge impact on me was one that wasn't popular was I Think I do. Not only does it have the adorable Alexis Arquette staring in it, it also has some great one-liners in the script and doesn't talk down to gay youth in the way some movies do. It moved me and had me on the edge of my seat and I couldn't wait to get the DVD. I love the acting in it and I love the happy way it makes me feel at the end. It is a must in any gay DVD collection." **Kevin, Horley.**

29

Sebastiane

Director: Derek Jarman, Paul Humfress.

Starring: Barney james, Neil Kennedy, Richard Warwick, Leo Treviglio.

This was Derek Jarman's debut feature film and it created a real hullabaloo when it was released over the extremely unambiguous, unadulterated portrayal of homosexuality, violence, and the eventual martyrdom of St Sebastiane.

Compelling, vibrant and striking are just three words that have been used to describe the opening of this film in which Jarman offers up an unforgettable sequence of Roman excess and Bacchanalian sexuality. You know right from the outset this is going to be no shrinking violet, no wilting wallflower; it is a vibrant and flaming forest of creativity. There are so many influences here it's hard to know where to begin, but I suppose the most obvious ones would include Ken Russell's The Devils, Federico Fellini's Satyricon and Cecil B. DeMille's The Sign Of The Cross. I love the shade, the light and dark, the whole feeling and the seemingly free movement of the camera offers up the best of the visually stunning scenes.

Sebastiane, played by the devilishly handsome Leonardo Treviglio, is a good friend of the emperor and captain of his guard, a high rank indeed. Stands accused of defending a Christian, and is quickly demoted in rank to that of a mere soldier. He is then further punished by being banished from the excesses of Rome to a lonely isolated coastal outpost. It is an incredibly remote and barren place, little more than distant wasteland. However, this very isolation offers solace in the freedom the men that inhabit this outpost are able to enjoy. They can and do explore hidden sexual desires, and homosexual fantasies become realities. Sebastiane angers the little outpost's captain by spurning his sexual advances and devoting himself to Christianity. It culminates in a violent but touchingly potent homoerotic ending that is a cinematic treasure of its age.

This really is one of the few films that turned gay cinema into an available art form and should be treasured as the landmark in the history of gay cinema that it is. It was made and came out in the seventies, a decade when boundaries were really being pushed to extremes, not just in the movies, but also in society as a whole. Sebastiane is no different; it rampantly pushes homoerotic imagery into the forefront of the camera lens and made a brave and ultimately triumphant stand against the censorship of the BBFC, the British Board of Film Classification, which was in the most part successful. An erection was cut but most of the kissing, touching, caressing and love making remains intact, or as intact as Jarman himself intended it to be.

There are great moments of extreme closeness and eroticism, that lift this film to higher levels and transport it from just a gay movie to a great gay movie and it remains so to this day. With words in Latin and English subtitles and music by Brian Eno it really was an exceptional piece of movie making. There are moments of pure pleasure, lust, longing, sadness and sexual tension but there are also moments that make little sense or are overplayed, yet they are in the minority.

For some it might not stand the test of time, it might look dated, people will criticise various aspects of the film and it's making, however that may be more to do with what we are now more used to, the CGI, the rapid edits, the action at breakneck speeds, the one minute fifty second scene and the acceptability of homosexuality, both in society and cinematography. However, that said, it will always remain an important keystone of gay cinema in the UK and therefore its influential standing is guaranteed.

"One film to nominate, a one word title and a one word description – Sebastiane, magnificent." **Albert, Milton Keynes.**

"Derek Jarman's Sebastane must surly be ranked highly in the top influential gay films, it may have been made a long time ago, 75 I seem to remember, yet it pushed the envelope to the max of what was and was not acceptable. I don't think we had ever seen so much naked flesh in a film that wasn't illegal pornography at the time. It also showed homosexuality and homosexual love making in a way that was entrancing, erotic, and powerful." **Alexander, Paris.**

28

Summer Storm / Sommersturm

Director: Mark Kreuzpaintner.

Starring: Robert Stadlober, Kostja Ullmann, Marlon Kittel, Hanno Koffler

A fabulous enchanting European coming of age and coming out movie with appealing fresh faces and great countryside. Tobi and Achim are best mates; they have been that way for years. One is a cox and the other an oarsman and together they have helped power their little local rowing club to win several rowing cups over the years. Off to a big regatta the team goes, hoping to savour the rich taste of victory, which is, supposedly well within their grasp. However, nothing is certain and there is trouble in the German countryside, this is not going to be your usual summer camp experience. Achim's relationship with his girlfriend and teammate Sandra grows rapidly more serious, Tobi begins to realise that his feelings for Achim run a tad deeper than just friendship, yep he thinks he's got the hot's for his best mate. When Sandra's best friend Anke shows her interest our hero, his anxieties jump into hyper-drive and the young lad is super confused.

A powerful Berlin girl's team was due at the regatta, however much to the chagrin of many of the teenage boys; they cancel and are replaced by another team – Queerschlag. Queerschlag as you might have guessed by the name, even if German is not one of your languages, are an openly gay rowing team who are going all out win the competition and have a little fun along the way. The appearance of some handsome gay guys adds even more fuel to the fire of confusion consuming Tobi. There are tears before bedtime, there is confrontation and there are a few sweet intimate moments when emotions are exposed to the harsh light reality and a summer storm.

This is a wonderful pleasing low budget movie that accurately and tenderly grapples with prejudice, fear, longing, sexual awakening and confronting sexual identity. Tenderly shot, thoughtfully played, honestly written and heart-warmingly authentic.

"Probably the best coming out movie ever made. It deals with the issues facing closeted gay teens with humor, sensitivity, reality and pure honesty. I

believe this should be a film studied in all schools around the film. Directed, acted, filmed and cast to perfection. Brilliant."
Jason King, film critic, Sydney.

"Simply the best coming out movie I've ever seen, it was so real it was like looking at my life on the TV screen. I love the way it was filmed, the scenery is amazing, the acting is great, the writing is spot on"
Nick, blogger, Birmingham.

27

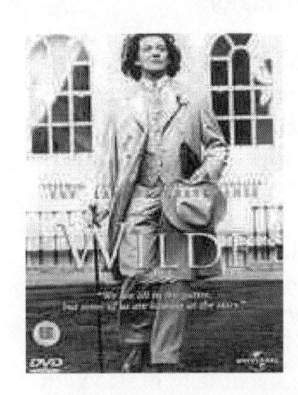

Wilde

Director: Brian Gilbert.

Starring: Stephen Fry, Jude Law, Vanessa Redgrave, Michael Sheen, Zoë Wanamaker, Ioan Gruffudd.

There can be no doubt that Oscar Wilde was virtuoso of the art of word placement; a brilliant poet, playwright, dramatist and public speaker. There can also be little doubt that there have been numerous plays, books and films about his life, however, few if any, are as authoritative, commanding and entertaining as Brian Gilbert's Wilde, starring the darling and equally verbosely eloquent Stephen Fry.

This is Oscar Wilde at his ultimate best, warts and all, presented in pure melodramatic biopic feature stance with a sensational cast of high quality consummate British actors that grace the screen with their presence and ability. Wilde, the film, came out during 1997, almost 100 after Wilde departed this earth and yet what a fine testament to his brilliance that we are still talking about and enjoying his work today.

Fry is a darling of British entertainment; he is without hesitation these days classified as a national treasure, that it seems almost absurd that at the time of production, it was hard for the producers to secure enough finance to begin production due to his lack of 'starability'. Yet, from the very first few seconds on screen, you can tell the casting was superb, Fry was born to play Wilde and Wilde was made so Fry could later play him, the two go together like breathing with living.

Back from his 1882 tour of Colorado Oscar Wilde marries Constance Lloyd and before you can earnestly prick up your portrait in the attic, bash out a couple of sons, as was the way back in the day. While their second sprog is just month's old, the couple play host to a dashing young Canadian, Robbie Ross, who somehow manages to seduce Oscar Wilde, helping him come to terms with his homosexuality.

During a little shindig of an opening night, Wilde is re-introduced to the dynamically handsome Lord Alfred Douglas, the most foppish of all fops, played sublimely by Jude Law. Thus the two fall into a bout of mad, passionate, tempestuous love. Alfred, god love him, is not, and who could really blame him with a face like that, the monogamous sort and frequently enjoys the company of working renters, sometimes with dear old Wilde taking on a role as voyeur and even perhaps sex commentator.

The evil Marquess of Queensberry, Alfie's dear old daddy objects to his son's on-going relationship with Oscar, so he badmouths him in public. Oscar sues the Marquess for libel, but in doing so his homosexuality is publicly exposed. Opps indeed, eventually tried and convicted for gross indecency he is sentenced to two years' hard labour.

His little wifey doesn't divorce him, instead takes their sons to Germany, informing Wilde he is more than welcome to visit just as long as he never sees Alfred Douglas again. Oh what to do, how difficult life becomes when tangles first appear. Oscar goes straight into exile in continental Europe after his release from the evil goal, but against all advice eventually meets with Alfred again, and that in a potted nutshell is an abbreviated biography of this biopic.

I am not sure how true this is, but apparently, Orlando Bloom made his first ever film appearance as one of the rent boys in Wilde, which only goes to show what an amazing job they did of casting this modern masterpiece of British drama. Everyone seemed to love Stephen Fry as Oscar Wilde, Kevin Thomas of the LA Times said the film "has found a perfect Oscar in the formidably talented Stephen Fry" while the SF Chronicle gushed "Stephen Fry has the title role, and it's hard to imagine a more appropriate actor". Many sighted the obvious similarities between the two men, size, shape, sexuality and absurdly sharp, stunningly fast wit and a worldly epic vocabulary.

Wilde was everything the critics said it was and far far more besides, meaning many things to many people, not least a study aid to hundreds of thousands of English students the world over. It may be hard to review a film such as this, because in doing so, are we really not also reviewing Oscar's life in some part, which many others have completed, far better than I could ever. Yet not to include it in a top listing of influential gay films would be a much greater travesty, such is the impact both have had on the lives of many.

"For me Wilde is a sympathetic yet honest reassessment of Oscar Wilde's life and times, Fry is wonderful and so like Wilde, being a gay intellectual. Jude Law was Alfred Douglas as no other person could be and he's made his career on the back of this movie. Tom Wilkinson received hate mail, so good is he as the Marquess of Queensbury. Perhaps too much time was spent on the 'sensational' aspects of Wilde's life, however it still magnificently portrays one of the greatest gays of all time" **Ian, Drayton.**

26

The Boys In the Band.
Director: William Friedkin.
Starring: Kenneth Nelson, Leonard Frey, Cliff Gorman, Laurence Luckinbill, Frederick Combs, Keith Prentice, Robert La Tourneaux.

William Friedkin directed this classic 1970 American drama often cited as the original foundation film on which the entire gay cinema genre stands. Mart Crowley wrote The Boys in the Band as a play, which was staged on Broadway for a good long while, before he adapted it to form a screenplay, the basis of this film. The Boys in the Band was one of, if not *the* very first major movies to feature and revolve around gay characters. This has always been seen as a milestone in the history of gay cinema and lauded as such, which I will not argue with in the slightest. It undoubtedly does hold a special place within the collective heart of the gay movie industry; it is a piece of queer movie history, which should be cherished for that reason alone. I was no more than an Action Man playing sprog during the seventies and only saw this film as a closeted curious fourteen year old in the mid-eighties and in all honesty I can only say it absolutely depressed the hell out of me. It also scared me a great deal; I feared that was how I was going to end up, a bitter, self-loathing, horrible, unfriendly and ultimately lonely person. I had few other gay role models to show me these characters belonged to another time and were so far removed from my life as an Umpa Lumpa. It is hard to see The Boys in the Band now as anything other than a dated and flawed example of gay life in depressing pre-Stonewall New York. Yet, perhaps that is slightly unfair, yes it is extremely dated, although as writer Mart Crowley stated in various interviews at the time, he wrote this in the late sixties when homosexuality was still considered by many as a mental illness, that going to gay bars of an evening was likely to get you arrested in a police raid. He also testified that he knew many people like the 'boys' he depicted in his play that ran from April 1968 to late September 1970. When it came out as a move, will all the same cast as performed in the play, it was already in danger of being a period piece, yet because it was played so well by an incredibly talented and experienced cast, it emerged as a vital document of gay social history and comment. It opened to mixed reaction from the critics, most had a muted acceptance of it, some offered a few lukewarm compliments while others disliked it. The reaction of the LA Times was typical of the homophobic discrimination of the day when they refused to carry ads for the film.

The film, like the play takes place almost solely at Michael's plush Upper East-Side apartment in New York City, sometime in the 1960's. Kenneth Nelson plays Michael; a recovering alcoholic catholic who is hosting a birthday party for one of his pals, a guy called Harold, played by Leonard Frey. Other friends at the party include underachiever Donald, Alan, Michael's straight (oh yeah?) former college roommate, camp Emory, a rather effeminate interior decorator. Straight acting Hank and Larry are a couple, ones a schoolteacher and the other a fashion photographer, then there is Bernard, a black bookstore clerk and a rather dim male hustler Cowboy who has been hired as Harold's birthday present.

They talk, drink, slating each other in the process and a sudden downpour forces the 'happy' party crowd inside and the conversations take on a more barbed and less friendly tone. There follows a truth game, where each of the 'boys' has to call the one person whom they truly have loved. Each call opens up old scars, hidden anxieties and reopens old wounds. It is not always pretty and it is not always clever to open up old personal lacerations such as these and the self-loathing and bitchy behaviour of this group of friends is sometimes rather painful to endure. Some of the behaviours are still present in today's society, if you do not believe me, just pop down to your local gay bar on a Saturday night or Sunday afternoon and you will see similar characters. Just open your eyes and they will all be there, the campy queens, the guys that fire bitchy barbs and savage put-downs to the very people they call friends, the straight acting couple with roving eyes not for each other, the not so clever lad living on looks rather than brains at the end of the bar or by the door. Yet we have moved on, the self-pity, self-loathing, bitterness, denial and perhaps some internalised homophobia have all become less and less stereotypical feelings applied to all homosexuals. Social acceptance, equality, pride and gay festivals have all played their part in changing the way we as a gay society not only look to others, but also look and feel to ourselves.

I am not going to lie and say watching Boys in the Band is as easy and as pain free as a walk in the park on a summer's day. It is not, there are some real poignant and embittered moments, which sting like crazy. However, it is also a rewarding experience, it shows you how far our society has allowed us to be, an insight on times gone by, whilst enjoying the emotional and actual freedoms and acceptance that we now have.

"The Boys In The Band was the first gay movie I ever saw, I have to say it had a profound effect on my life, for sometime I went back into the so called closet, I was afraid of my sexuality, because I didn't feel bitchy, I wasn't good at design, I didn't feel depressed about myself, I wasn't that good at thinking up really fast negative remarks about people and I was afraid to do that. The Boys In The Band showed me that is what I should expect my life to be like." **PS, Surrey.**

"I wasn't born when the film Boys In The Band was made and I don't know what life must have been like back then for gay people, I know it was hard, really hard for some more than others which makes BITB so important. It helps people my age understand about the problems gay people had to go through back then. It has some well funny lines, like going blue from rimmin a snowman, and serious things like how hard it is to be a gay and religious. Yes it is old, but it isn't dated as lots of the same issues still are around today." **Ben.**

"The power and emotion displayed in every scene of The Boys In The Band is a real treat to watch, they are so comfortable around each other that they deliver lines so perfectly weighted with depth, meaning and timing. It touches on many issues and is incredibly sad, so many neuroses, fear and inner loathing in one room has rarely been seen. Although it is rather inward it is also outward because you cant leave at the end of the film without thinking positive things about your own life." **Seb, Southampton.**

"The first major gay movie, deeply emotional and ferociously scripted The Boys In The Band is the most influential gay movie of all time. Had it not been for this movie, there possibly would not have been a whole decade of gay movies that followed. It recreated life on screen for many older gay people of the 60's and 70's a world before AIDS. Sad to know that five of the main cast of the film all died of AIDS." **Pierre, Lyon.**

25

Bent

Director: Sean Mathias

Starring: Clive Owen, Lothaire Blue, Sir Ian McKellen, Jude Law, Mick Jagger.

An intriguing and stimulating cast is bought together for this cinematic recreation of Martin Sherman's deeply affecting thought educing stage play. Set during the dark days pre-World War II, in a rough Berlin, handsome Max, played dourly by Clive Owen, is a vaguely promiscuous hedonistic gay guy, isolated from his rich family due to his wayward ways and his overt homosexuality.

He and his partner Rudy are caught up in the mass hysteria and horrific marginalisation of the Nazi segregation and inhalation programmes and are forced to flee Berlin. Sir Ian McKellen, playing a kindly uncle can arrange false papers for Max, but not for Rudy. Incidentally, Ian McKellen was also in the original 1979 play version in London's West End. Max cannot leave his vulnerable lover behind and the long and short of the matter, they are caught and are placed on a train to a concentration camp. Horrific brutality from the guards and deeply unpalatable self-preservation behaviour is exhibited on the train and Rudy is killed.

Max manages to lie and bribe his way into being labelled with the yellow star of the Jewish rather than the pink triangle of the gays and is set to work in the prison camp. It is an extreme life of hardship and pointless tasks, yet in this austere and stagnant backdrop, he falls in love with fellow prisoner, Horst. A tragic tale of emotion, love and dignity at a time of great suffering, which brings together an interesting cast including Jude Law as a storm trooper, Rachel Weisz as a whore and oddly, Mick Jagger as a dire drag queen who is bizarrely good. Lothaire Bluteau and Clive Owen are tremendous in the two lead roles and there is bound to be tears before bedtime.

"love, romance, hatred, discrimination and above all, pride are all featured in Bent with such passion it is both painful and entertaining to watch." **Amy, Brighton.**

"Bent is an amazing film, it really takes hold of your heart and rips it through your chest" **Anon**

"I adore Bent, mainly because I think the story is so powerful and so damaging. Excellent acting by Clive Owen and Lothaire Blue as Max and Horst and you so wanted a different outcome for them. It is amazing what people will do for love and also what they can't do for it" **Jess, Norwich.**

"A wonderful play about doomed love, transferred to film in an accurate and moving way. Bent has got one of the most enchanting non-touching love scenes ever made." **Andy, Sussex.**

24

Shelter

Director: Jonah Markowitz.
Starring: Trevor Wright, Brad Rowe, Tina Holmes, Ross Thomas, Katie Walder.

Shelter is an award winning 2007 debut feature by writer, director Jonah Markowitz, often dubbed the 'Gay Surfer Movie' by journalists and reviewers alike, in much the same way as Brokeback Mountain was labelled the 'Gay Cowboy Movie'. It is essentially a love story between a couple of guys doing what they love, surfing and spending time outside, and considering they come from California they have a lot of opportunity to do that.

Trevor Wright plays Zach, an aspiring artist living in San Pedro, which is a pretty working class suburb of Los Angeles. He is essentially a nice guy, he has put his dreams of art school on hold for a while as he helps his family out. Taking care of his older manipulative sister Jeanne, his little nephew Cody and their disabled father takes up a fair amount of his time. To make ends meet he works in a restaurant cooking fast food and when he gets some free time he likes to paint, draw murals, surf, and hang out with his best mate Gabe. He also finds time to see his quasi-girlfriend, their relationship seems to be one of those off again on again off again affairs, both not quite ready to cut the cord completely and they really understand in an unspoken sort of way it is more friendship that relationship.

All is sedate revolving and unaffected until Gabe's older brother Shaun comes down for a few weeks and as Zach and Shaun go surfing together a friendship grows and develops between them at thunderous speed. Shaun, played by the lovely Brad Rowe, encourages Zach follow his dreams a little more and take control of his life. Confusion starts to rage in Zach's mind, his emotions are all in a state of flux, which is only added to when one evening after an afternoon of surfing Shaun kisses Zach. Whilst it is a pleasurable experience for them both, Zach is not quite ready to expand and explore the feelings the kiss has given birth to. It takes a little while, but a little soul searching later their friendship soon morphs into a full on romance, all the while Shaun builds up a strong rapport with Zach's little nephew, Cody.

There are some lovely comic moments spaced throughout the movie, for example, Zach and Shaun are in bed together after a bit of bonding, when they hear Gabe coming back from college, which results in a rapid hiding of Zach, which could have easily turned into loose farce had the scene pacing been carefully thought out.

Sister Jeanne knows Zach has been spending a lot of time with Shaun, she warns Zach of Shaun sexuality and telling him to keep Cody away from him. This brings in the obligatory social pressure needed to further confuse poor Zach. Does he focus on family obligations or his emerging relationship with Shaun or even to work more on his dreams of going off to art school? Oh, it is all so confusing, so muddling, thank goodness there is the beach and the sun and the surf!

Behind the scenes, Shaun has been a bit of a mischievous minx and secretly submitted an application to art school on Zach's behalf. This is the movies, so as you would expect, this clandestine application gains Zach an offer of a full scholarship. Yay for Zach, yay for Shaun and yay for everyone really. However, we are not quite at the happy ever after stage yet and there is more malarkey on the horizon to deal with. Jeanne's boyfriend, the rather nasty Alan gets a job in some godforsaken place; I think it is called Portland, which is so not within LA commuting distance. Therefore he has to move and wants Jeanne to come along too, there is a bit of a ruction between him and little cute Cody, which peeves the hell out of uncle Zach and the two have a little set-to! The short and long of this aggravation is that Jeanne leaves Cody with Zach and Shaun and pushes off with her boyfriend to a new life in Portland, what a nice mother she is.

Sometime later, we see Cody, Shaun and Zach on the beach and you get the impression it is a happy ever after for the gay couple and their semi-adopted son. How bloody perfect is that?

Talented Trevor Wright plays the young sexy Zach with an incredibly intense ability and honesty that he lights up the screen with his performance. I also like Brad Rowe as the handsome slightly older Shaun and there is a real sense of closeness between the two when they occupy the same screen, which only adds to the enjoyment factor of this rather sort story of love in the sun.

The film scored a slew of awards from various GLBT film festivals, including best actor and best cinematography at Tampa, best film at Dallas, best feature at Melbourne, best director at Seattle and GLAAD honoured it with an outstanding film award in 2009.

It is a sweet and gentle romance with a heart and an interesting core whilst also not being too adventurous, left field or controversial. Some in the cruel light of a dank, drizzly English morning might proffer Shelter is as tame as an episode of Iggle Piggle's In The Night Garden, so packed is it with typical clichés and soft soaping of the issues that it should stay as a teatime special on Hallmark or Really. However, not all gay movies need to be gritty, dark and depressing; sometimes it is nice to have light, jolly and a happy ending. In addition, this one has some stunning scenery and eye candy to take your mind away from the plot inadequacies or the soft storyline. It is true; one of the reasons for Shelter's mass popularity must in part be due to the wonderful cinematography employed throughout this sunny LA creation. Those waves, that sand, those clear skies and oh, that abundance of flesh on display all add to the general enjoyment factor. Thank you're god or guru for the fact that the main cast are rather pretty and cannily remain topless for so much of the films duration. Yes, it is more than just a gay surfer movies, but you know, there is nowt much wrong with a gay surfer movie, dude, even if it is not so rad!

"A wonderful coming to terms with your sexuality, falling in love, achieving dreams and playing happy gay families film, which has a happy ending and some great outside shots. Oh to be on that beach!" **Drew, Margate.**

"Shelter is a brilliant amazing film about love, family and relationships which is so anti-brokeback type of film. It is a genuine lovely story about gay love and relationships. How it starts, how it builds, how they grow and how anything is possible. I love the scenes with Zach and Shaun, they seem so easy together that you think they are a real couple. The difficulties of family obligations and relationships are shown really well, realistic as well, not all happy all the time." **Kelli Dee, San Diego.**

"Shelter has got to be one of the best gay movies I have seen, I highly suggest this for your compilation. The direction of the movie is superb as is the photography and the cast are simply wonderful, you can't fail to like them. Good story, lots of drama, a few jokes, lots of love and perfect combination of all four of those. It is truly enjoyable and not at all like being preached to, like some other popular gay movies tend to do." **Gerry, Anaheim.**

23

Happy Together

Director: Wong Kar-wai.

Starring: Tony Leung Chiu-wai, Chang Chen, Leslie Cheung.

Happy Together is a deeply dark tortuous movie written and directed by Wong Kar-wai that was mostly filmed on location in Argentina during 1995 and 96. Kar-wai wrote and re-wrote it many times and re-conceived various parts of the story repeatedly during the shooting of the movie, straining both patience and health of both cast and crew. It proved to be a very long and troublesome film to produce, partly due to the subject matter and party the lack of financial backing. Moreover, it has been said they even ran out of good film stock during some stages of the production, yet the result is stylish, provocative and visually dramatic.

It may not have been a mega box office smash hit, yet it remains an intensely passionate cinematic gem which scored no less than seventeen award nominations, winning best director for Kar-wai at the 1997 Cannes Festival, best cinematography for Christopher Doyle during the 1997 Golden Horse Awards and best actor for Tony Leung Chiu-wai at the Hong Kong Film Awards also in 97. Critics the world over seemed mostly enthralled by it, especially the symbolic, ultra gritty innovative cinematography and impressively free and stylistic directorial approach.

Dark, moody, corrosive, sullen are just four word that could jump into a paragraph or two to briefly describe this moviemaking motion picture treasure of supreme aptitude and standing, Stylish, emotive and humbling are just three more than just tumble from the tip of my tongue when even the mere mention of the title of this film is uttered. Happy Together is anything but a happy together tale of life, it is far more destructively deceptive and altogether realistic than a plastic pop tune of the sixties might suppose. It is a film that demands and commands attention right from the very start and the edge of the seat only is released from temporary imprisonment after the end credits have become but a memory.

Ho Po-Wing and his rather promiscuous lover Lai Yiu-fai have seemingly run away from a pre-Chinese handover Hong Kong and have found themselves visiting the South American nation of Argentina where they wish to secure a much more stable basis for their troubled relationship. They also have a major goal for this South American exploration and that is to reach the Iguazu Waterfalls, which is a floating theme throughout the movie.

They arrive in Argentina pick up a hire car and head for the capital Buenos Aires, however along the journey they row and split up. The volatile fiery relationship is a major theme of the movie, it is a pattern of abuse, argument, break up and eventual resolution. Sometimes painful to watch, deeply affecting, yet captivating and compelling rather like a cut or sore that you just can't leave to heal and are constantly picking at the scab and prodding the oozing flesh.

Lai is the more rational of the two and in reality just seeks a normal routine sort of life; he deals with the break up in his typical understated and rational way and finds himself a position at a local nightclub. Ho is fiery, explosive, destructive, manipulative and lacks the ability to be monogamous or even committed. He often frequents the nightclub that Lai works in, showing off the various men he has hooked up with. Lai is struggling incredibly hard to maintain a normal life and at this stage is almost driven to distraction by Ho's antics.

The atmosphere and sentiment is enhanced by the impressive cinematography employed by Doyle here with a realistic environment that is both exciting and depressing in equal measure at the same time. One day Ho arrives mashed and beaten at Lai's one room apartment, with nowhere else left for him to go. Lai, the caring fool that he is, takes Ho in and starts to care and look after him, attending to all his needs. Lai battles hard to retain the status quo however, eventually they get back together. It is a short passage of time before the ultimate behavioural pattern of their relationship remerges, abuse, argument, break up and reconciliation. Ho slowly recovers from his injuries and as he does so, he picks up random strange men and even takes them back to the tiny apartment.

The relationship is tumbling out of control and is incredibly destructive and painful, yet Lai turns his attentions elsewhere. He becomes friends with a young Taiwanese man, Chang at work. Chang is kind, considerate, stable, normal, all the things that Ho is not and Lai begins to spend more and more time with the handsome young gentleman. Ho in the meantime has pretty much resumed his rather hedonistic playboy sort of life, where he gets the cash from is not immediately apparent, but it is not from working hard that is for sure. Chang and Lai find out through their discussions and conversations that they are in somewhat similar situations, both at a crossroads in their lives. Lai wants to see the falls whilst Chang needs to go to a lighthouse at the lowest point of the world, where you can free yourself of all your sorrows by throwing them off the top. They inspire each other and Chang departs Buenos Aires to continue his journey to the lighthouse at the lowest point of South America.

Lai sinks into a deep depression once Chang has departed, however he takes on some different unsavoury jobs, such as doorman, cook and abattoir worker in order to earn more money. He relieves some of his stress, depression and tension by meeting the occasion man in gay cinemas and in public toilets. It is a coping mechanism, helping to heal and mask the emotional turmoil and devastation he feels within him. Writing a letter home over Christmas proved to be a cathartic experience for Lai and he vows to make amends for his past actions and return to Hong Kong. Lai resolve is strong and he even refuses to even see Ho when he come to ask to move back with him, it is an incredible break for previous behaviour and is empowering to observe on screen. We really have witnessed a metamorphosis so much, so that Lai has the strength to visit the falls on his own, make it back to Hong Kong, although on the way he stops in Taiwan to visit Chang's parents noodle stand in a market in Taipei. He steals a photograph of the handsome Chang and head on his way back home.

This is no walk in the park type of movie, nor is it glitz glamour and drag queens aplenty, it is a hard-hitting gritty passionate tale of evolving love and internal courage to break free from a cycle of devastation and destruction toward a more hopeful tomorrow. A movie metaphor for anyone living in a destructive relationship if ever there was one, although it is much more than just a metaphor it is a damn near dramatic instruction manual.

Top marks and much kudos to the three core cast who are so honest and pure to the characters they are completely believable in their parts, which considering they are quite big stars to say the least in the Far East is no easy task, so hats off to them.

In Cantonese, what little dialogue there is, with English subtitles, it relies more on visual communication to tell the story of this troubled most unlikely of gay couples, who start off with little or no back story to convey to the audience. It has powerful images, gentle music, harsh visions, deep emotions and a broodingly affecting voice-over. There are some intelligent movie making choices in action throughout from sudden freeze-frames, shrinking frames and slow motion when little action takes place, just as a mind remembers things in times gone by. Combined with the slightly odd and disjointed colour matching, slippy snippy editing and flashes of black and white emphasis this is not your run of the mill gay teen flick. It is one level painful to watch the destructive relationship playing out, on another it is beautiful, cinematically atmospheric and visually stunning. It's depth alone make this film influential, it's subject matter and the way a dysfunctional gay relationship is presented is completely different than we're use to and as such exerts another chuck of influence on future filmmakers and directors. Another demonstration of the stimulus of Happy Together is demonstrated by the effect it has on the audience, I have yet to meet anyone who has seen it that has not been moved in some way by it, which is the mark of a good movie.

"Happy Together is one of the greatest films I have ever seen, which have been many, it is one of the most disturbing gay films I think I have experienced in the last 20 or so years. We're not used to this sort of reality and darkness in gay themed films relationships that are so fractured and fragmented you wonder why the couple are still together. The isolation of these two oriental men in a foreign land is emphasised by them not often having much to say or do with the locals, except sex. It breaks away from the expected 'gay' issues, such as someone coming out, someone dying of aids, someone struggling to get married or someone doing drag on stage. This is real, this is as it should be, this is life. Some people will not be able to cope with the seriousness of the films central core, yet Happy Together is a masterpiece, a true masterpiece". **PS. Surrey.**

"No ordinary love story, no ordinary cast, no ordinary movie, very influential Happy Together is anything but happy." **Chris, Peckham.**

22

The Broken Hearts Club

Director: Greg Berlanti

Starring: Dean Cain, Nia Long, Timothy Olyphant, Zach Braff, Andrew Keegan, Mary McCormack, John Mahoney, Billy Porter, Justin Theroux, Ben Weber, Matt McGrath

Every stage and age of gay life is here in this neatly packaged 'romantic comedy' movie which In all honesty was surprisingly good and oddly poignant. Written and directed by Greg Berlanti who had previously written episodes of the popular American teen television show Dawson's Creek, could have been kitchen sink teen soap drama material. However, this slice of American gay life focusing on a close-knit social group of gay guys in the hot and vibrant West Hollywood, California has much more depth that you would have thought possible. Throughout the movie, we watch as this group of guys with very different personalities, tastes and ideal support and care for each one another. There is Howie who just cannot seem to let go of his ex-lover Marshall, even after Marshall starts to date another guy. There is the dashing narcissistically challenged Cole who would uses men like play things, carelessly throwing them away as soon as he's done, until he falls for someone, who literally throws him away. Patrick is another member of this band of friends; he has self-worth issues and must decide if he can pass on his sperm to his lesbian sister and her partner. Benji works hard on being accepted at any cost by the muscly dudes he admires so much, but the costs are high. Just at the start of his gay life, coming to terms with his sexuality and heading toward his first gay experience is the adorably cute Kevin, who touches a few hearts. The various stages of a break up are all consuming for the charmingly sweet Taylor and all this is set against the local gay softball team from Jack's Broken Heart's restaurant. Jack is the father figure of the group but ultimately the real lynch pin holding it all together is Dennis. Now Dennis is an aspiring photographer with a great eye for a shot and a caring personality that the others sometimes abuse yet love. Tragedy strikes this wonderful little group of pals and they come together for support, for love and for strength.

One of the best things about this film is the way it shows all the various stages of gay life, the important things we all seem to go through, from the coming out, the exploration of our sexuality and our feelings. There is the self-conscious period, the shag anything period, the times when a relationship just will not work, yet being single does not seem to work. A wonderful poignant yet funny film about friends who love, support and annoy the hell out of each other.

The script is wonderfully written, with powerful and funny lines side by side delivered by a wonderful ensemble cast, including Superman Dean Cain and Frasier's dad the lovely and talented John Mahoney. It had a low budget and was shot at a very rapid pace, which perhaps shows in one or two places, however the enjoyment factor overrides these slight flaws. It's not a rite of passage movie, or a film about AIDS, nor are there drag queens at every turn and you'll be hard pushed to find embittered angry parents, which may surprise you, this being a gay movie and all. Yes, it is a romantic comedy, yes it is a gay romantic comedy and yes, it is a bloody good film.

"Not an award winning film, but hugely enjoyable with believable characters in believable situations at various stages of their lives." **Betty, Redhill.**

"At first I was a little sceptical however after the very first viewing I found myself looking at myself at various times over the last thirty or so years. Broken Hearts Club is a true to life comedy with a good helping of romance and just a little pathos, the same as life. I found it incredibly enjoyable although the lesbians should have either had a more meaty role or been edited out, as they added little to the story as a whole. That said, it still portrays gay life in a positive way, it was also nice to see an older gay gentleman in a happy and stable relationship and accepted by the younger gay community." **Al, London.**

21

My Own Private Idaho

Director: **Gus Van Sant**

Starring: **River Phoenix, Keanu Reeves, James Russo.**

Gus Van Sant essentially takes on Shakespeare's Henry IV; it featured the aesthetically delightful River Phoenix as Mike Waters, a wonderfully apt narcoleptic male whore who we first get a glimpse of tipping down an open stretch of road in Idaho. Mike and the action shifts from the cold Seattle to equally cold Portland. It is here that he makes friends with Scott Favor, a secretly soon to be rich guy who is also on the game played by the often-maligned Keanu Reeves. The future for both is as uncertain as uncertain can be, will Scott take up the inheritance he about to get, will Mike survive the streets with his narcolepsy?

Mike feels real affections for Scott, however Scott refuses to believe men can really love each and it would seem that Scott is only doing the gay whole whore thing to kill time and get back at his family. Mike believes Scott will continue with the grand life on the streets, turning tricks even after he bags the inheritance; such is the allure of the unknown. There are many of fellow working boys who agree with Mike's view.

This is an uneasy picture, a colourful and surreal attempt to really take the characters to a different kingdom. At times, it is a wonderful although slightly glossy take on the real street hustlers shagging their way to oblivion or not as the individual case may be. Drug abuse and risky behaviours are commonplace on the streets and in the world of the male hooker and it is a small feature of this sometimes-disturbing film.

The character of Mike seems almost apologetically plausible, abandoned as a child and obsessed with finding his real long lost mother. Scott less believable as the rebellious disillusioned spoilt little rich kid gone rebelliously bad. You really would not have put them together by design, but fate disregards those lines and together they embark on a quest to find Mike's mother, from Portland to Idaho to Italy they do travel.

There is no argument the cinematic quality and the unbelievably stunning settings help to make this film an intriguingly striking viewing delight. It is exceptionally well thought out in terms of location and setting and a master-class for any would be cinematographer. The characterisation I found to be impressive, even Keanu Reeves played his part with just the right amount of smug pathos and humour, especially with the flippantly arrogant lines afford to him. River Phoenix works pure magic on screen with this performance and I am fairly sure I'm not alone in believing this is the role that set him into the great immortal movie star hall of fame. It is no wonder that he pulled in a number of 'best actor' type awards for this intrinsically faceted role. His campfire scene, in which Mike declares his love for Scott, is much applauded by audiences and critics alike – Newsweek claiming it to be "A marvel of delicacy" it really is a testament to what a wonderful talent River Phoenix was, because he wrote that part of the script himself. Village Voice said, "Phoenix vanishes with reckless triumph into his role". It earned around £5 million at the box office worldwide, which is quite impressive, more than that in video and DVD sales.

My Own Private Idaho takes the spirit and passion of Shakespeare, bends, manipulates and shapes it to find form in a more modern setting, which works beyond expectation in the most part. Although the traditionalist in me seems to hold the opinion that you should not mess with old Shakey and if you do, you best be prepared to face the harshest of critics. Adaptations are always open to personal interpretation and modifications, which others may not agree with, like or even accept, yet this one seems to work and seems to be commended as a job well done.

"My Own Private Idaho, is truly a remarkable and a completely different release for its time. It was the first art house commercial film I can remember that blended a brilliant art house story and director with two of the hottest and talented actors for their time. It was a massive risk for both actors and one that has benefited them immensely."
Jason King, Film critic, Sydney.

20

Juste Une Question D'Amour

Director: Christian Faure.

Starring: Cyrille Thouvenin, Stephan Guerin-Tillie, Eva Darlan.

A beautiful emotive portrait of love between two people who are opposite ends of the coming out process coupled with strained family relations and emotional upheaval. With broad-brush strokes and delicate touches of colour and humour Juste Une Question D'Amour, gets to the heart of human emotion in a pure and faultless way. There is an refreshing honesty in the characters and storyline that really is a joy to watch, especially as it navigates well clear of the supposed stereotypes that can often dog other releases from the gay cinema industry. There are no drag queens, no leather men, no simpering disco dollies with their heads in the clouds and no randy bears lusting after the next young cub to wander in sporting check shirt and dirty Levi's. Nope, this is so not that sort of movie, there are just ordinary people here, just nice average ordinary folk and it is so much the better for it.

A heart-breaking portrait of suburban and rural French life, Juste Une Question D'Amour follows two weeks in the life of Laurent, a fascinating young French guy in his very early twenties as he navigates some difficult personal circumstances and decisions. Laurent's family are hideously beset with deep-seated homophobia, Laurent's own cousin and childhood best friend, Marc, was completely disowned and ostracised when his sexuality became known. The entire family, with the exception of Laurent refused point-blank to visit Marc in hospital before he died.

We see Laurent's family, his father and uncle talking about how homosexuality disgusts them and his grief weary mother is seems to be walking through life in a zombie like state, so consumed is she by her own thoughts, her own grief who swallows half a drug store each day just to get by.

Laurent has unsurprisingly and understandably retreated away from his own sexual identity, as well as his family to some extent. On the occasions when he does visit, he is never alone, he takes his friend and roommate Carole with him. Carole is a bright and obliging girl, who will happily masquerade as his girlfriend at times like these although even she is getting weary of the duplicity, especially as Laurent's parents seem to think the two will eventually get married.

There are some beautiful moments between Laurent and Carole that are light, easy and yet so full of affection and care they are a joy to watch and had Laurent not been gay, you know they could have made a lovely couple.

Laurent's education in horticulture is suffering as a result of his family's attitudes and his cousin's death, his grades are falling and the only way to salvage his college career is to agree to a brief internship. This brings him head on with Cedric, a dashingly appealing agricultural scientist who has a laboratory next to the garden centre he manages with his mother. They also live together in a lovely little house beside this idyllic garden centre.

Beautiful scenes follow as the two young men get to know each other, explore the others personalities, ideal and dreams. There are moments of pure tender reflection, infectious affection, laughter and just a little pain. Laurent is amazed and secretly impressed with the open attitude of acceptance by Cedric's mother, she bat's not an eyelash, let alone lid, at her sons sexuality. So far removed from his own first hand experiences, it opens his eyes and his mind a little further, expanding the realm of possibilities.

Cedric's mother is a deeply feeling and intuitive person, she is also refreshingly honest and makes no bones about the fact that she wishes her son were straight, yet as she calls it, it is better for her son to be gay and part of her life, than be gay a not part of it. The mother-son dynamic works incredibly well here and they are such believable characters that you cannot help but feel drawn and warm to them. The affection, care and love is clear to see, enjoy and almost taste.

Laurent firmly believes he will never be able to attain such an honest, open and respectful relationship with his parents, he remains firmly in the closet. This both angers and annoys Cedric, who does not want to and almost directly refuses to pretend to be something that he is not, which leads to tension and an argument, in which their fledgling relationship is torn asunder.

Cedric's mother does not want her son to be unhappy and heart-broken again and you get the impression she has the same feelings toward Laurent, that whilst Cedric is away in Paris, she decides on a little trip herself. Off she drives to the country village where Laurent's parents run a little drug store. Once there she tells them she wants their help to get their two sons back together. Now there is some ambiguity surrounding her knowledge, did she know Laurent was not out and therefore forcing the situation, or did she genuinely believe he was as open with his parents as her son is with her? Either way, the news that she brings is not welcome and goes down like Gary Glitter shopping in Mothercare!

Laurent is beside himself when he finds out what she has done, it is all his worst nightmares arriving at once. His head and heart are pounding yet answers are far from his confused mind. His parents are equally as distraught and muddled and you recognise there is going to be much soul searching and tears falling before bedtime.

It is an achingly poignant and deeply affecting movie for its realistically honest depictions of human relationships in the crux of death and revelation. It shines a light on the scenario or situations that many gay people go through on the 'coming out' bus journey. It affectionately and decently deals with a range of views and emotions, without ever getting confused. It is also a film about love, first love, real love, family love and friendship love and what each of those mean and how they make us react and engage.

There are wonderful moments of pure romantic joy combined with full on delicious angst and everything in between in a script that is both cutting and loving at the same time whist executed with such precision, grace and style. Every character in this French cinematic pleasure appears genuine, believable and portrayed with such wonderful total trustworthiness. Particularly the two leads, Stephan Guerin-Tillie and Cyrille Thouvenin as Cedric and Laurent. Not only are they aesthetically gorgeous, but you genuinely believe they love and care for each other. It is rare that you can find two actors that seamlessly move through the range of relationship emotions yet retaining sincerity, decency and believability such as these two effortless maintain.

I adore this films beauty in its entirety, not just the intelligent script, but also the outstanding actors, the striking locations, the honest sentiments, the stereotype free portraits of homosexuality, the forever-evolving relationship and the warm afterglow emotions. It is clear to see why over six million French people tuned in to watch this movie when it was first broadcast. Oh didn't I say it was a made for TV movie? Well, it was, although you would never have known that just by watching it, so astonishing good just a question of love is.

"Just A Question Of Love is the very best film I've ever seen about coming out and gay love." **Stu, Cork.**

"This is one of the most positive films involving gay people and homosexuality I have seen in a long while. There are no people dying of AIDS, there are no effeminate flamboyant characters, there are no predatory older men, there are no street hustlers, there are just positive role model normal homosexual people going about normal occupations in normal life. Very few films have such positive roles and positions for homosexuals. It is exquisitely performed by a hardworking cast who should have been rewarded for their performances. Love comes in many forms, this picture indicates that fully and should be celebrated." **Alexander, Paris.**

"The French have a knack of taking a nice story and making it work in screen and Juste Une Question D'Amour is a clear example of that. It is wonderfully filmed, lovely surroundings, very pretty cast – who could not fall in love with Cedric? Or be pleased with his mother's acceptance of his sexuality and lifestyle? They take a coming out story and make it more three dimensional that any other film of the same subject. Usually homophobic bigots either stay that way or have a sudden dramatic epiphany and change at the click of fingers. Life is not like that and neither is Just Une Question d'Amour, you see the situation from all sides, with no unrealistic conversions. It is touchingly real and a must see movie." **David, Chester.**

19

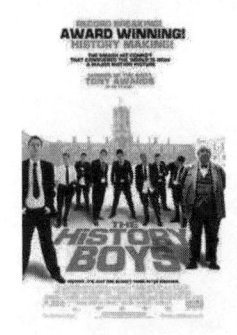

The History Boys

Director: Nicholas Hytner.

Starring: Richard Griffiths, Frances de la Tour, Samuel Barnett, Dominic Cooper, James Corden, Jamie Parker, Russell Tovey, Sacha Dhawan, Andrew Knott, Samuel Anderson.

The History Boys, a wonderful stage comedy by the legendary Alan Bennett remained the toast of the National Theatre long before it was taken to the big screen, by Bennett himself. The complete cast reprised their stage roles for the cinematic version, before they headed off on a brief world tour with the play. In New York the play won an astonishing colossal five Tony Awards, the crème de le crème of Broadway's theatre scene.

A group of eight boys, the product of a northern state grammar school of the mid 1980's who achieve the highest A level results the school has ever known. They now have a realistic chance of passing the infamously difficult Oxford and Cambridge entrance exam. It is a major achievement for both the boys from a state school to get that far, but if they could pass, well that would be a magnificent success story for normal working class lads from the north. This exceptional film details the relationship these boys have with the three teachers tasked with getting them ready to face the entrance exam, interview and life in within the upper echelons of the British educational system. First, there is Hector, a loveable wonderfully inspiring yet slightly uncontrolled and free spirited teacher who cares more for their happiness and the joy of learning rather than their academic futures. Lintot or Totty, the second of the teaching trio, is a more traditional educator, her approach is all facts, facts, facts, history is all facts and then, she is kind, she has got them so far already, but perhaps something exciting is lacking. That missing excitement is delivered by new teacher Mr Irwin hired with the express intention of getting the boys up to the Oxbridge standard.

There are magnificent scenes acted out by a cast so comfortable with each other, believing they are actors and not school boys on the verge of greatness is difficult in the extreme. They play off each other, spark each other and work with each other with astonishing ease leaving you the peace to be able to enjoy the unfolding story, rich in literature references and human emotions. A wonderfully amusing scene in which the boys act out a scene in a French brothel entirely in French, leant phonetically by the actors, yet so perfectly balanced and accentuated for Sheffield schoolboys.

Magnificent Richard Griffiths plays eccentric Hector who enthuses about literature, learning, growing and maturing, he tries to install that love of everything creative into his students. He also likes to give them a little ride on his motorbike and surreptitiously fondles them, they have become accustom to his wandering hand, however they simply dismiss his attention with a disdainful 'oi' or a shrugged removal. However when a nosy lollipop lady notices something amiss and reports him to the head. The long and short is that he has to hang up his teaching hat at the end of term and take early retirement.

We follow the boys as they take the entrance examinations, which were phased out in the late eighties, head off to interviews at the various university colleges in Oxford or Cambridge. This is a wonderful stimulating film that says as much about the feelings, emotions, learning and maturing of the teachers as well as the boys. The superb script is pure classic Alan Bennett, packed with wit and charm in spades. The sage honest humour peppers the dialogue like school being the opposite of prison – 'At school you don't get parole. Good behaviour just brings a longer sentence'. Those delightfully chosen words, those reflections of languages and subtle nuances of expression are a true delight to hear and enjoy in a script created by as some might say is the Wilde of our time. The cinematography works so well, despite the lack of numerous settings, chases or rapid action shots. There are however plenty of moving shots around the classroom, in and round and around the boys, giving a real sense of being there, almost enabling you to touch the boys and smell the chalk dust and stale aroma of school. An added layer of authenticity derives from the realisation that for most of the action in the movie was filmed in a couple of real schools in Watford. Exterior was the boy's side of Watford Grammar school and the interiors were done on the girl's side. It is partly this 'realistic' or natural additive, which increases the charm of the entire wonder that is The History Boys.

Critics mostly enjoyed the movie version of the play, the New York Magazine said it was 'Brilliant and infectious' Hollywood Reporter claimed 'Bennett's achievement is not so much to take sides as to let the three teachers and their charges to have their say'. It was The Observers film of the week 'Alan Bennett's The History Boys is special' they said and I most certainly would not disagree with that. The Beeb said 'slightly fusty but wickedly witty'. 'Quick, raunchy, reflective and bittersweet" said the Austin Chronicle whilst Jason Korsner said it 'not very cinematic'.

Alan Bennett's words are enchanting, witty, frank, picturesque, and combined with a cast of brilliant young, and a couple of not so young, actors, they make The History Boys a joy to watch over and over again. Richard Griffiths is such a fine actor or immense stature and standing, that he owns the role of Hector, his face so full of dramatic expression, his voice curls the words in to a dance. Frances de la Tour is a triumph as downcast and droll Mrs Lintott who has delivered embittered yet unrealised lines 'History is a commentary on the various continuing incapability's of men. What is History? History is women following behind, with the bucket.' Moreover, the best 'Can you, for a moment, imagine how depressing it is to teach five centuries of masculine ineptitude?' you just have to love her, you do honestly.

Dominic Cooper is the supposedly handsome hunk of the class, so convinced of his sexual heat and attractiveness he defies anyone not to want him, even Irwin. The openly gay student Posner is played so incredulously well by Samuel Barnett you just want to give him a hug and assure him that this too will pass, so perfect is he. I am so glad the movie version has a much better end for him over the play's rather savage and hauntingly sad penned life. He may not be happy but he's not unhappy about that and at least one of the class is passing it on. Russell Tovey as the slack, lax and coasting Rudge, an unnoticed character of immense proportions, who is just trudging along, not really caring if he will get there or not, it is only toward the end you notice this and realise the little looks and vacant expressions have been there all the way through. Jamie Parker as Scripps is amusing, entertaining and one of the stronger stoic salt of the earth types, a friend to everyone and everyone's friend. Then there is the effervescent James Corden who really shines as the tubby Timms, such an amalgamation of such vast talent all in one place is rare, very rare indeed.

"The History Boys is pure joy to watch. It is a fabulous example of British filmmaking" **Martin, Horsham.**

"One of the best films in recent times has gotta be The History Boys, written by Alan Bennett. It deals with all the big issues, sexuality, humanity, history, learning, education, ambition and the fragility of the human soul. It reaches in and takes hold of everything, gives it a good old shake and lets it all out again, but in a different order. It is like the English version of Dead Poets Society, just with a little harder edge to it. Sadly it's reputation is being severely tarnished because of a campaign to post negative and factually inaccurate reviews on internet sites like Rotten Tomatoes and IMDB by religious zealots who haven't seen the film. So many people will miss out on great entertainment" **George, London.**

18

La Cage aux Folles

Director: Edouard Molinaro

Starring: Ugo Tognazzi, Michel Serrault, Claire Maurier

La Cage aux Folles film was a wonderful major international comedy drama sensation based on an incredibly successful French stage play of the same name. It is a brilliant comedic faithful recreation telling the beautiful story of gay couple Renato Baldi the manager of a Saint-Tropez drag nightclub and Albin Mougeotte, the star attraction playing it straight for Renato's son Laurent seems omitted these many facts like this from his future father-in-law. His beloveds' father happens to be a big wheel in a morally conservative political organization and would not be over the moon for his daughter to marry a young guy with two gay men as parents. Not wishing to ruin his son's chances of happiness, Renato agrees go straight, at least for a little while. Yet a lifetime of gayness does not just vanish overnight, plus there is the difficulty of getting Albin to adopt an air of heterosexuality and masculinity. However, Albin comes up with the inspired idea of him adopting a more conservative style of the drag he's used to and posing as Renato's wife. It could be an ideal situation, but things do not all go to plan with almost farcical complications cropping up at every turn.

La Cage aux Folles was an exceptionally forward film for its time and presented a highly camp way of life, which for some audiences was quite a surprise. Considering this film came out in 1978/79 when homosexuality and female impersonation was nowhere near as accepted as they are in our more enlightened and accepting times, its success is very extraordinary. In part, I think this is due to the wonderful jollity of the piece, the unthreatening central characters and the abundance of both spoken and visual jokes. Mainstream audiences enjoyed it, gay audiences loved it and a big hit it went on to become.

 Ugo Tognazzi played Renato with superb style whilst Michel Serrault took the role of Albin/Zaza to the extreme and headed the wonderful ensemble cast, whom for the most part also dubbed the English language version from their native tongue. Although I would suggest the original version with the subtitles if you want to fully experience the exquisiteness. Every member of the cast play their parts honestly and directly and form the meat of this entertaining film which unlike so many others, doesn't flag or seem overly long or indeed padded out with filler. Due to the subtle funny and comedic style, the tender moments of which there are a few tend to stand out, however they are played so well they stand up to the extra attention admirably and the film is better for them.

There are so many issues at play here that the films influence is quite often under estimated, however thing for a moment and consider how many plays give birth to films that are so good they run for a year in some cinemas, inspire two popular remakes and spurn on a play that runs for over one thousand seven hundred performances?

The abiding message of accepting diversity is a key part of this wonderful cinematic creation, long before 'embracing diversity' became an overused phrase of equal opportunity policies the world over. It was, perhaps a long way ahead of its time in that respect, yet it is a message that still holds strong today.

"The wonderful La Cage aux Folles holds many memories for me, for people of my generation it was probably the first time we saw a gay couple, drag queens and female impersonation on the big screen as the main characters and not the amusing butt of jokes cameo parts that were more usual in those days. I can remember going to see it at the cinema and loving it so much I went back the next night and the next." **George, Kent.**

"The most influential gay film? 'La Cage aux Folles' scores highly. The guys at first sight are seemingly all stereotype, but as the story unfolds they are revealed to have such love and compassion that they make mockery of their apparent stereotype." **Alec, Cambridge.**

"I loved the Birdcage, but I loved the original, La Cage aux Folles much much more. I first saw this as in the early 80's when I came out. It was a revelation to me, to my life and to my friends. Later when I had a VHS copy, we used to have La Cage parties, we'd all dress as one of the characters and watch the film and recite the lines along with the actors. Such fond memories, such wonderful times, although outside it may not have been the same." **John, Bletchley.**

17

Get Real

Director: Simon Shore.

Starring: Ben Silverstone.

This is one of the best gay coming of age drama's to come out of the British movie industry in recent times, well if 1999 can be considered recent? It created quite a stir on the film festival circuits including Edinburgh, Toronto and Sundance. Pulled in acclaim and derision in equal measure from that odd bread of human called movie critics, yet were not quite so divided and loved this kooky British story of love and coming out from 1999.

Sixteen year-old lanky Steven Carter is a boy with a secret, he cannot tell anyone he likes boys and not girls, except of course his slightly chubby best pal Linda, who seems old before her years. Oh and the occasional older bloke he picks up at the various public bogs around town, just to add that sleazy aspect to gay life that movies like to hit with. He wants to be a writer (Don't we all sugar!) and is already on the school newspaper team.

He also cannot tell anyone that he has the hot's for John, the school hunk and head boy, who without out a doubt would be called a jock if this were an American made picture. He's the sporty handsome guy with prospects that your mum longed for you to bring home after school or before a date, except he's straight. John's current squeeze is a model, but he is not short of admirers, seems the whole school get moist whenever he is around.

Before long, John and Steven finally meet, not at school, but in the cubicle of the local cottage, weird, odd, yes, I mean how many times do you strike up relationships with people you bump into during a random fumble in the dirty park bogs? However, hey, this is fiction and these sorts of things happen, besides, it helps the story develop and I am not being harsh, just honest. So anyway, as I say they strike up a friendship away from the seedy toilet sex and I don't mean swapping Match sticker cards at break time either, it's a full on love fest. However, this is Britain, supposedly modern times, this is school and John is supposedly straight, so they've got to keep their little romantic liaison secret, but as we all know, with secrets come lies and deceit and what a tangled web we weave when trying to keep our private life away from public eyes.

There is a lovely little scene at the school prop when they dance with each other with their eyes alone, in reality, they are dancing with their respective prop dates, but their eyes are locked on each other, which is both touching and oddly strange. However, things all work themselves out in the end, with a few little spills along the way. It really is a nice little film, even though I seem to knock it a bit, it has some important messages, not least when it raises the spectre of homophobic bullying and the harsh bitter reality of classroom taunts and sports field aggression. Dark and light go together in this film, with comic moments and serious situations simmer along side by side quite nicely. There are some weak jokes in the script that reply on old and overused campy gags you would expect from Julian Clary or Graham Norton.

Not often will a films DVD cover give the whole game away, usually it's just a slight flavour, but Get Real seems to not want you to watch by spelling out in American lingo most of the films plots and interests on the cover 'What if you can't avoid sexuality, guilt, peer pressure, lies, bigots, rumours, misunderstandings, nerds, jocks, romance, loneliness, shame and insecurity? Your only choice is to get real. School's out and so is Steven Carter.' It is such a shame because you know it has already put half the audience off, and that is the half that would really benefit from seeing it.

Get Real is a lovely film, some key issues are brushed upon; other's mysteriously absent, but on the whole an engaging movie of surprising depth. It has the ability to make you laugh aloud at the funny bits and tear up at some of the not so happy bits. I am sure the appeal of this movie has much to do with the reminiscent quality its storyline evokes in much of the collective minds of the audience. Many of us have had similar experiences at school, dealt with the same crap and overcome the taunts and teen angst as we battled our way through the choice of either staying safe and ultimately unrewarded in the closet. Alternatively, risking the abuse, possible gay bashing and isolation of coming out and being the only gay in the school.

"You gotta have Get Real in your list, it is the best gay movie about coming out in school in England. It kinda saved my life, allowing me to be me." **A teenage schoolboy twitter follower.**

"One of my favourite movies of all time has to be a rite of passage/coming of age/coming out film called Gat Real. It was realeased in 99, although I never heard of it at the time and only say the DVD about four years ago. It is all about coming to terms with your sexuality, falling in love and coming out whilst at school, which most people seem to have done. It is realistic and touchingly similar to my own experiences. I find myself crying my eyes out at the end, it is really moving." **Anthony, Devon.**

16

Latter Days

Director: C Jay Cox.
Statting: Wes Ramsey, Steve Sandvoss, Rebekah Johnson, Jacqueline Bisset.

This roller coaster of a movie has you up one minute almost wetting yourself with laughter and then almost blubbering like a schoolgirl into a snotty hanky the next. Put simply it is a modern day gay love story, but it is so much more than that, taking a look at uniting love from different sides of a religious divide as it does. It had mixed reactions from the critics when it was released in 2003/4 and barely broke even on the production costs, yet it garnered many awards from various lesbian and gay film festivals from all over the world.

Briefly Latter Days is the love story of Aaron Davis, played by Steve Sandvoss and Christian Markelli acted by Wes Ramsey who come from different sides of the religious tracks, so much so that it might as well be different worlds. It's these seemingly insurmountable differences that provide the bulk of the films content, substance and emotion. Aaron is a young Elder of the Mormon Church Of Jesus Christ Latter Day Saints, yep a Mormon missionary, he desperately wants to do his family proud and is quite passionate about his religion, he's also passionate about film. He is sent to the big bad city of Los Angeles with three fellow missionaries to preach the word of god, Mormon style. These three men of 'god' move into an apartment next door to Christian and his roommate Julie, who are both waiters with dreams, she's a singer and he's a err party boy!

At first glance, Christian seems a rather shallow character who only looks forward to shagging a new guy every night. This shallow and emotional carefree existence is amplified no end when he makes a $50 bet with a work colleague that he will bed one of the three newly arrived missionaries before the end of the month. He works fast and latches on to Aaron, the most inexperienced missionary and makes an assumption he has a closet gay guy. Now there are a few problems from here on for the two heroes of the piece, firstly Christian is falling for Aaron, secondly Aaron thinks Christian is a shallow 'shag anything' sort of guy and thirdly, most importantly the Mormon church doesn't do gay very well.

What follows is a tangled tale of battles and woe as first they are discovered in a romantic clinch and their love and sexual identity is forced out in the open. A cavalcade of emotion erupts for the two, as they have to go through the emotional ringer with things like regret, loss; perseverance, forgiveness and courage which all vie for mental headspace. Is it going to be a happy ending, can love conquer such a vast religious divide? I suppose you will just have to watch the film to find out, all I will say is it is a well-crafted picture laying emotion down thick, fast and heavy and really should have got a better reaction that it originally amassed. The story is well written and put together in a completely honest, frank and believable way. There are several issues raised during the course of the movie regarding not just gay, but any relationships where such a religious obstacle and difference is in place. For me, the movie only works because of that, take it away and you are left with little more than candyfloss. It is a passionate little film, with a passionate and powerful story to tell and I am so glad they made it. The Toronto Sun said it was "The most important gay movie of the last few years" whereas the LA Times chimed in with "At once romantic, earthy and socially critical. Latter Days is a dynamic film filled with humour and pathos". I for one cannot argue with those sentiments for as I said before the film is a bit of an emotional roller coaster. Gary Booher of Affirmation – a lesbian, gay, bisexual and transgender Mormon organisation praised the films accuracy "It was so realistic that it was scary. I felt exposed as the particulars of my experience and of others I know was brazenly spread across the big screen for all to behold" Those thoughts are echoed the bucket loads of positive comments received from former Mormons, excommunicated from the church because of their sexuality. It really is a powerful and honest emotive film about a subject that is not often covered in gay or even mainstream cinema.

"Beautiful, sad, comedic, soul searching, heart grabbing film. I pissed myself with laughter, I cried with emotional tearing and I shook with sobs at the end. The acting may not be the best in the world but it feels real, it grabs you and holds you and takes you on a journey you would never have expected." **Jason King, film critic, Sydney.**

"The acting isn't always spot on but the story is, it unexpectedly moves you to an emotional place when you least expect it. I was surprised by this film in many ways, the way it was played, the honest content, the confrontations and the music, which is exceptional. I've watched it many times now and each time it still moves me to tears." **James, Fort Lauderdale.**

"I am one of those ex-Mormon's excommunicated from the church because of my sexuality, it was a devastating and incredibly difficult experience to live through. And, there were many times during it that I seriously thought I wouldn't make the journey to the other side. I know of many who have not been as lucky as I. Which is one reason why this film is so important, it shows that there is life for gay men after the church, there is hope and happiness.

I never expected to have one of the biggest battles of my life recreated on the screen with such honesty and emotion, but that is what I got with Latter Days. For that, I am eternally grateful."
Anderson, St George.

15

Priest

Director: Antonia Bird

Starring: Linus Roache, Tom Wilkinson, Robert Carlyle

Young Father Pilkington, assigned to a central Liverpool parish is alarmed to find it's left-wing radical priest having a sexual tryst with the housekeeper. Not only that, but the senior Father is also battling and bickering with the bishops and church over issues of liberation theology amongst others. Pilkington is, despite his young age, a rather traditional conservative sort of priest; his religious and personal beliefs take a serious knocking by the older priest's blatant and wanton disregard of the celibacy vow. However deep inside Pilkington are his own demons, he is struggling with issues also of a sexual nature, only this time of the orientation kind. Father Pilkington is struggling to come to terms with his homosexuality and things get even more confusing when he embarks on a relationship with a chap called Graham that he meets at a local gay bar. Father Greg Pilkington then listens to student Lisa confided she is a victim of sexual abuse by her father, who, separately confesses to sexually abusing his daughter, but both are revealed in the confessional. That means Father Greg is bound by Catholic honour and the sanctity of the Sacrament of Penance from revealing what he has learnt. It is a secret he must keep, regardless of the suffering and emotional anguish being caused, and he tries to warn the girl's mother, obviously without giving away any details. Sometime later, the mother finds out what has been going on and verbally attacks Father Pilkington, who is sorrier than he can say. Things are not going well for the young priest, he gets arrested for getting up to a bit of jiggy jiggy with Graham in a parked car. If that wasn't bad enough, the local newspaper does not hold back after Father Pilkington pleads guilty and his peccadillos plastered all over the front page, it is so not a good time for the rather handsome troubled priest. He tries to relocate to a different and remote rural parish, however the Father there is beyond disapproving and unforgiving and all bar forces him to return to inner-city Liverpool. There is deep division in the parishioners over a gay priest, just as there is in the church, which is hammed home by the end scene of this controversial film.

The Catholic League for religious and civil rights was so outraged by this film they called for all of their members to boycott it and all other products from Disney. The Catholic Church in Ireland sought to have the film banned and battled with the Irish film censors, who eventually let the film come out with an 18 certificate. It deals directly with the hypocrisies of the Roman Catholic Church head on, from remorselessly casting aside vows to god, upholding the seal of secrecy of the confessional condoning as it does incestuous sexual abuse, denunciation and dismissal of homosexuality and homosexuals. A clear part of the story here in Priest is that according to the catholic church it is ok to sexually abuse your daughter, as long as you say a couple of Hail Mary's afterwards. Sin is awful and bad, unless of course, it is the priest doing it and then, hey it is all right after all. There are some impressive performances at play during Priest, not least Father Greg Pilkington – Linus Roach and his love interest, Graham played by Robert Carlyle. They are compelling to watch as they compassionately confront the situations they they must endure in the story, a real triumph of ability. Tom Wilkinson who plays the old and sinning Father is absolutely wonderful and chilling at the same time, such is the authenticity of his performance. The gritty realism aspect is perhaps not surprising as the screenplay was written by none other than Jimmy McGovern, so you know it's going to have more layers than an onion and just the same amount of bite.

"Priest was one of the most controversial films of the 90's, it challenged the whole catholic system at the core out. It was confrontational, explosive and deeply routed in the hypocritical way the church works. The light it shows on priests living double lives should be cheered, yet the church tried to ban it, which should tell you more about how good it was." **Ann, Dublin.**

"Better than Brokeback, more passionate than Priscilla and more honest than Philadelphia. Priest got loads of bad publicity at the time, mainly from catholic church bishops and the religious right who probably hadn't even seen it. They really missed out, it is not all about bashing the church, or priests, it is about human relationships and the difficulties in overcoming our own and well as societies hang ups and approvals. It is not about how bad religion is, it is about how bad some peoples two-facedness and double standards are. It is dramatic, powerful and emotional. It really tells a story and one not glossed up or made to be pretty for the cameras, it shows life who life really is, dirty and depressing. It is a challenging watch but a rewarding one at that." **Tim, London.**

14

Another Country

Director: Marek Kanievska

Starring: Rupert Everett, Colin Firth, Michael Jenn, Cary Elwes, Anna Massey.

A magnificent enchanting and deeply touching tale of class and hypocrisy surrounding the young inhabitants of a history English public school. This is a highly moving expose of the supposed teenage school days of infamous spy Guy Burgess is rich, deep and luxurious. It is aesthetically pleasing with authentic although slightly mixed locations and the moody atmospherics employed heighten the enjoyment factor no end. The running undercurrents of class, breeding, expectation and tradition are the key features of this moving and entertaining story showing the underbelly of a traditionally British educational establishment.

Rupert Everett stars as both an old Guy Bennett in a small apartment in snowy cold Moscow recounting his school days to a young female writer as well as the fresh faced young man he was in 1931. His performance bristles with the authenticity of class and ability. He is perfect as the too clever by half and defiantly too clever for his own good schoolboy Guy heading toward his last year of school, hoping to receive the adulation and power of school god. Such dizzy heights seem well within his grasp, after all, this is what his entire school days have been building up to, plus it's the level his ancestry achieved in generations gone by.

His best friend is the broodingly attractive Marx reading communist loving Tommy Judd, played with skill and passion by the young Colin Firth, already demonstrating the skills that have taken him to the very top of the British acting profession. Guy and Tommy are friends, mainly because they are on the outside of the establishment, in that they simply don't follow the accepted norms of behaviour. Guy simply for his open homosexuality and Judd for his communist Marxist leanings and beliefs. Their friendship is one of surprising depths, based on mutual respect and affection, a respect that would later have far-reaching implications.

The public school setting of the 1930's could really be anywhere in the United Kingdom and at any decade of the last one hundred and fifty years or so, such is the timeless charm of tradition, still played out in many schools up and down the country to this day. A master on his way somewhere hears a noise and stumbled upon Martineau, an endearingly cute blonde haired lad and a boy from another house engaged on a sexual act in one of the school changing rooms. It is a mutual act, which we are lead to believe is commonplace in the darker places of a school of this type and time and is usually ignored, a blind eye turned to it. However, there are no blind eyes when it comes to the masters and Martineau faces expulsion for the most scandalous of reasons, a fate he just cannot allow to endure. Thus, the poor troubled boy takes his own life in the school chapel.

Master and pupils alike are aghast at this course of action and they must pull together to prevent a scandal striking at the school, for all their sakes, they pull ranks and tighten the positions and time to rule with a rod of steel. What follows is essentially a power-based annihilation of homosexuality that may or may not be prevalent in each house of the school. Bennett, who is rather more open than most about his preference, is subject to increased scrutiny and investigation. The unspoken message seems to be that no gay boy will be allowed as a school god; it is a simple as that.

Meanwhile, Bennett has fallen head over heels in love with a blonde blue-eyed lad called James Harcourt, whom he invites to lunch and has the most amazing time getting drunk with. He adores the young man in such a pure and passionate way. Bennett is punished for something, however manages to escape a serious beating by telling the gods if he were to receive the caning, he'd let out the names of all the boys he'd had sexual relations with over the last four years to the masters, effectively blackmailing more quite a few of the house.

However, a second time, for fear of compromising James Harcourt, he succumbs to the beating, which is delivered, as is usually the case in films of this sort, with an over the top sadistic enjoyment by the head of house.

Dealings and double-dealings surrounding just who will reach the dizzy heights of school gods next term. The despicable end result of this dealing and backstabbing denies Bennett the sought after dream of 'god' status.

Bennett is completely devastated by this turn of events; he had built his whole future around becoming a god and then going on to work in the diplomatic service before becoming a British ambassador. His whole world is crashing around his ears and he finally opens his eyes to the realisation that the British class system is built around shady corruption hidden by a supposed honourable outward appearance, the veneer of respectability. No commies and no queers!

It becomes abundantly clear to him that an openly homosexual male, whom had not amassed the ranks of school god, would have little chance of climbing the career ladder in the diplomatic service; dreams of being called ambassador are left crushed and broken. 'Wouldn't it be wonderful if communism were really true' he muses to Judd after it's made clear the gods are out of his reach, 'it is true assures Judd, earth on earth, the just earth, it seems so beautiful, so idealistic as the sort haunting music stirs under them walking across the quad.

Of course, Tommy was killed in the Spanish Civil war, the elderly Guy tells as we head back to the cold confines of Moscow and the home of the former spy.   Little touches of dear old England abound the tiny apartment, a mug from Harrods, tea, Johnny Walker black label and the little mementoes of a time long since passed, black and white photographs of lives left behind.

It is an incredibly well made film, full of evocative images, fantastic settings added to by Michael Storey's simply extraordinarily redolent musical score, reinforcing the melancholic retrospection of incredulous depth that this film encapsulates so magnificently. With a period piece such as this, authenticity and atmosphere are mandatory for success and Another Country has this in spades.

The film was cleverly adapted by Julian Mitchell from his award winning play of the same name and came out in 1984 and was itself nominated for three BAFTA's. Both Firth and Everett had starred as Bennett in the stage play along

101

with a host of other notable names of the British acting elite, Daniel Day Lewis and Kenneth Branagh to name but two. There are some major differences between stage and screen versions, the actual appearance of Harcourt for example; the story is essentially the same, told with equal passion and melancholia. The audience is always left to wonder just how close the film and play came to telling the actual school days of the legendary Cambridge spies of Burgess, Maclean and Philby, which is, I suppose how it should be. Although I would chance an arm and suppose that, some parts were not dissimilar at all. Oh, a little interesting side note is that a very young ninth Earl Spencer is one of the background artists, in a number of scenes, yes; a little Charles Spencer is an extra in the movie, I wonder what his big sister, Diana, thought about that!

"Another Country has always been a wonderful example of understated British gay movie making. It is all about homosexuality and the British class system, which, especially in terms of school days, go hand in hand. Another Country is a wonderful taste of that life. It might not have been successful as a lot of other gay movies, especially more recent ones, yet it holds a special place in the memories of many." **John, Milton Keynes.**

13

Parting Glances

Director: Bill Sherwood

Starring: Richard Ganoung, John Bolger, Steve Buscemi, Adam Nathan, Kathy Kinney.

Parting Glances was made in 1984 and had a somewhat limited release in 1986 and is without a doubt a powerful and important film in the genre that is gay cinema. It was one of the very first American films to feature the then relatively new disease of HIV/AIDS at a time when much was still unknown about the disease and prejudice against it was at its highest. Bill Sherwood, the writer and director passed away from an AIDS related complication in 1990, Parting Glances was his first and last film

The main aspect of the story focuses on a New York gay couple, Robert and Michael, in their twenties. Robert is heading off on an incredibly long assignment for the World Health Organisation to deepest darkest and most isolated Africa, Michael, his partner, is staying behind. The film is set out over the two days prior to Robert's departure, with some scenes taking place at an amusing farewell party hosted by the couple's friend, Joan. Some other scenes take place at a dinner party thrown by Richard's unconventional boss and there is a whole bulk with Nick, an old friend and ex-lover of Michael's who happens to be living with AIDS.

That is a much-condensed highly abridged synopsis of the film, which has been classified as a drama but contains so many touchingly funny moments you could be forgiven for labelling it a comedy-drama or a dramatic comedy. One of the delights at the time of its release was the unashamed way it blasted on to the screen, almost screaming out, I am here, I am queer and I am not conforming to your stereotypical ideas of a gay movie. It opens with a tame, but in your face, love scene between Michael and Robert, which demands you sit up and take notice and you know this is not just some usual comedy flick. The fact that Bill Sherwood choose to put the sex up the front is a masterstroke in making the movie more about the relationships than the sex. It also illustrates that this is not a strange coming of age tale, these are not freaky off the wall odd gay's, these are your run of the mill normal average Joe, American gay next door type gays, refreshing and very welcome. The script is fun, witty, exciting and interesting, some of the lines given to the character of Nick are so sharp they cut the dialogue like acid through skin, they really are that potent. There are many different character types populating the movie, especially at the party scenes, which show off New York's society rather well and make you hanker for a live in Manhattan in the early eighties.

Parting Glances was one of the first movies to deal with the subject of AIDS in such a frank, direct and honest way, which for the time was a real revelation. It did not gloss over, nor shy away from the implications or the savagery associated with the disease, at a time when everything like it was still new. There are some deeply searching moments, not least when Nick talks of the decadent and hedonistic days back in the freedom of the seventies creeping into the early eighties. This low budget but important film was made on a budget of a couple of dollars over $40,000, which in movie terms is not even the shell on a peanut. The shooting was completed in a whirlwind seven days, which is remarkable to say the least, you'd certainly not think it was made that quickly when you watch it. I am fond of this movie, it may seem a little dated at first, but then we are going back almost thirty years since it was made, so it is bound to show some signs of age. Yet, through an exceptionally shrewd script and some talented acting the complexities and nuances of the human relationships shine on the screen, yes even now, after all this time, they still have the power to move. I would suggest a couple of viewings are required to get the full impact of this film to the innocent virginal viewer, otherwise you might not catch some of the intriguingly witty throw away lines peppering the dialogue.

"Quintessentially THE gay movie of the 1980's and probably of all time!" **anon.**

"Parting Glances is a brilliant film, it was the first gay themed film I ever saw, the first AIDS film I ever saw and it apologised for neither. It was a good representation of gay people in the 80's and before and was long before its time. It took on issues without being preachy or campaigning. It did not make jokes out of gay people the way other films and shows of the time did. It changed the way many people thought of gays, it also helped people understand more about AIDS. It made a difference to how gays were seen and also more importantly how we saw ourselves." **Michael, Boston.**

12

Director/producer: James Ivory, Ismail Merchant.

Starring: James Wilby, Hugh Grant, Rupert Graves, Ben Kingsley, Denholm Elliott, Simon Callow

Quite simply one of the most exquisitely cinematic explorations of gay love that has ever created produced by Ismail Merchant, directed by James Ivory and adapted from the classic E. M. Forster novel, Maurice is a true masterpiece.

A quintessentially English example of love between men in the early 20th century at a time when homosexuality was still illegal and persecution was everywhere. This delightfully considered and delicately fragranced tale starts with a windswept walk along the beach for an eleven-year-old Maurice Hall and his bumbling although well-meaning school master Mr Ducie, played by a darling of the British theatre scene and all round nice guy, Simon Callow. Mr Ducie tries to explain the rudimentary "sacred mysteries" of sexual intercourse with the aid of sand drawings to the fatherless young man on the very periphery of puberty.

Years later, in 1909, Maurice Hall is attending Cambridge, striking up friendships with aristocratic Lord Risley and the jolly lip smacking lovely Clive Durham. Durham, played by a devilishly handsome and not yet type cast Hugh Grant who seems to fall quite madly in love with the long tall blonde Maurice Hall, and who could really blame him. He surprises Maurice by fessing up to his emotions, which take young Maurice on the hop a bit. At first, he is muddled and confused by the declaration, yet soon comes to realise and accept he has similar feelings for his friend.

These two fresh faced undergrads embark in a love affair as dreamy as the university spires, yet the relationship remains purely platonic. To tread further ground would diminish them both, says Clive and you can tell Maurice, while he might nod along, he does not fully agree. Maurice is sent down, leaves under a cloud from the academic hot seat of Cambridge and yet, he maintains a strong friendship with Clive Durham. Maurice, with a little help, finds work embarking on an unrewarding career as a London stockbroker. A big fat spanner is thrown well and truly into the workings of a 'happy ever after' life when our two platonic lovers get frightened as university chum Lord Risley is not only arrested, but also sentenced to six months hard labour. His crime was supposedly soliciting sex from dashing army soldier, who may well have been up for it at the time!

Clive Durham has his future all planned ahead is afraid of being exposed as a homosexual, something that can't happen, so breaks with Maurice and after a while following family pressure marries a plain and naive young lady called Anne. Maurice is heartbroken yet also wants to rid himself of these homosexual yearnings and leanings, so seeks the help of a rather slimy therapist by the name of Lasker-Jones, who tries to cure him with hypnosis. It is not very successful, thankfully or there would be no story to tell, just the pieces to pick up of disentangled and wasted lives. Maurice and his aloof ways come to the attention of the supposedly uneducated under-gamekeeper working on Durham's country estate. How Maurice fails to notice the adorable Alec Scudder, played supremely by Rupert Graves is a mystery to all bar himself, yet the young handsome manly servant is not put off. One rainy evening a few nights later, Scudder risks everything and yet nothing by climbing a ladder and into Maurice's bedroom, they kiss and spend most of the night 'getting to know' each other.

After this first meeting Maurice receives a scrawled note from Scudder, wanting to meat in the boathouse, however, Maurice is suspicious by nature, particular in view of what occurred to Lord Risley and believes Scudder will try and blackmail him. He runs back to London and tries to cure himself, with Lasker-Jones' help. Poor Scudder is heartbroken, he heads off to the big smoke to find his blonde haired gentleman lover, which is a truly brave act considering the time and their respective places in society and class. They meet at the British Museum and after an amusing chance encounter with Mr Ducie they resolve the misunderstanding and head off to a cheap hotel. This is the first time that Maurice starts to use Scudder's first name of Alec, which is a beautiful and subtle moment.

Long-term joys are not on the horizon, in just a couple of days Alec Scudder is booked on a passage to a new life in the new world. Somehow, Scudder misses the boat, confusion reigns supreme for a good long while. Maurice muddled by everything confesses all to Clive Durham who understands little and off Maurice troots to the boathouse. Oh, the rapture and the wonder then he find dear young Scudder there, waiting for him. It's bewilderingly romantic and powerfully affecting, Scudder apparently sent a telegram to Maurice, though it was never received, informing him that he'd left his family and the chance of a new life overseas to stay with Maurice and telling him to come to the boathouse. They melt into each other's arms and the effervescent glow of love surrounds them in a bubble of happiness as Scudder whispers "Now we shan't never be parted."

Oh, how I wanted my own Scudder, or indeed to be someone else's Scudder when I first saw Maurice back in 1987 or 88, such was the magnificence and beauty of the story. The stunning production qualities, wonderful photography and cinematography in plump richness, exuberant colour with the finest of details all ensure this is one of the finest costume period drama ever made. Gay or otherwise!

Forster wrote this mainly between 1913 and 1914, yet it was only published for the first time in 1971 a full year after his death. Forster himself was reticent about its publication mainly because of the legal and public attitudes towards homosexuality at the time. Indeed, a handwritten note on the original manuscript allegedly said "Publishable, but worth it?" He wanted it to have a happy ending, not the one made up in the film version, but perhaps one of the Scudder and Maurice years later as a pair of woodcutters, having lived a long and happy life together, although this epilogue of sorts was discarded by Forster himself.

Many academic types, including those at Kings College, believe Maurice to be a substandard Forster novel, compared with A Passage to India and Howards End. They very nearly did not give permission for the film to be made, or indeed shot on location at Kings. Thankfully, they relented, and the world could enjoy a cinematic masterpiece, filmed in part, where Forster himself would have walked during his days at Cambridge.

James Wilby and Hugh Grant excel as Maurice and Clive; indeed many still believe this to be Grant's career best performance. Rupert Graves is magnificent as the beautiful Alec Scudder. In addition, there is a potent supporting cast including Denholm Elliott, Simon Callow, Billie Whitelaw and Ben Kingsley.

This movie had a profound impact on my early teenage years, not only igniting a love of literature but also in my acceptance of sexuality, profoundly moving, entertaining and liberating. There are parts now, even after all these years, still make me swoon and moisten my eyes.

"Maurice is a timeless classic, it is period drama, social statement, historic account, love story all in combined in superb pictures. The Merchant/Ivory production certainly does justice to E.M. Forster's words. The social stigma attached to homosexuality of the time it was written was still very much in evidence at the time of its release with Thatcher trying to outlaw homosexuality by the back door with the awful section 28. A year later, the book was withdrawn from many local schools." **Roger, Horsham.**

11

Longtime Companion

Director: **Norman Rene.**

Starring: **Stephen Caffrey, Patrick Cassidy, Brian Cousins, Bruce Davidson, Campbell Scott.**

Longtime Companion was perhaps one of the very first movies to put a face, heart and soul to the epidemic of HIV/AIDS at a time when movie makers as well as society as a whole, ran as fast as they could away from not only the disease itself, but also those that had it. For that, alone it should be congratulated and celebrated. Head on it tackled the issues without glitz or glamour and with an authentic honesty of emotion and interaction that is quite breath taking.

Essentially, Longtime Companion is the story of how life takes a sudden change for a group of gay friends from the very onset of the whole HIV/AIDS crisis in 1981. Back then the New York Times carried an article that mentioned an outbreak of a 'rare cancer' in the gay community, often termed 'gay cancer' which was tragedy in itself as it shielded the actual method of transmission of the illness that was spreading with alarming speed. During the film we travel with the group of friends from the streets of New York to the hedonistic freedoms of Fire Island where the mentality of 'it couldn't happen to me' 'you can't catch a cancer' ruled the heads of many.

Nobody was invincible and nobody was immune to the onslaught of this new horrific disease, which is exposed to the full in this highly charged and emotive film. Coming as it did in 1989/90 it was the first time that a vast majority of its audience had seen beyond the all too often misleading newspaper headlines, it was especially heart wrenching. There is not a particular plot line to follow, except watching with tear festooned eyes the lives of a whole circle of friends crumble and falter in the face of illness and death. There are few punches held back, nor emotions left unstirred as the action takes place at a reasonably fast pace. Many critics at the time had issues with the clinical approach of the piece, but those issues are unfounded and groundless.

Longtime Companion gives a wonderful vent to the sense of confusion, misinformation and huge sense of loss that existed at the time. It is only with the benefit of hindsight that we see how tragically accurate this was. I firmly believe this should have been mandatory viewing in secondary schools during the early nineties for the way in which it dealt with homosexuality, relationships, and the whole HIV/AIDS crisis from its early beginnings. It would have done so very much more than a pathetic iceberg and a strapline of 'Don't die of ignorance' that was pretty much all the UK got in the way of warning and advice. One of the amazingly beneficial aspects of Longtime Companion is the matter of fact style of presentation was see the story unfold, some have even said it a shadow of 'documentary' which is no bad thing. We see the lives of men cut down in their prime, of devastated lovers and partners, of a whole community decimated and challenged, which was exactly the reality of the age. No matter how many times I watch this movie, I still weep, I still find myself moved beyond words, I still find my heart aches and breaks a little each time, which for a movie is a fine testament. Yes, it may seem rather dated, especially with the acceptance and understanding we now have, along with the developments in treatment, but life hasn't always been as easy as it is today, which is demonstrated admirably in this film, that took over £3 million at the box office.

"I cry like a baby each time I watch it. It simply is the best film about aids there has ever been and I am included Philadelphia in that. It is honest and heart wrenching, it raises awareness as well as tells the intimate story of the struggles many of us faced during the 80's." **Steve, Aberdeen.**

"I can only recommend one film to your list of influential gay films and that is Longtime Companion. It was the first major film about HIV, long before it was called HIV, it dealt with issues in a way that was remarkably honest, accurate and devastatingly sad. To any of us that have lost friends or boyfriends to AIDS this film is a potent and candid account of that pain, sorrow and suffering. It is also reassuring in strange way, hopefully it shows how far we as a society have come, at least I hope that is the case. I doubt there will be many dry eyes at the end of this film." **Andrew, Hove.**

"The gay plague, that's how it was talked about in the papers and on telly when it first came about, a gay only cancer, that is what people thought, when Longtime Companion first came out, many still thought that. But that film quashed many rumours, lies and misconceptions. That makes it truly influential, I know it certainly opened my eyes to what the situation really was. I cried with my girlfriend when we first watch this together and having reciently watched it again, I'm not ashamed I stilled cried. Not many films make me do that! **Kevin, Hayward's Heath.**

10

Mysterious Skin

Director: Gregg Arki

Starring: Brady Corbet, Joseph Gordon-Levitt, Chase Ellison, George Webster.

Its summer 1981, eight year-old Brian Lackey is in a the crawlspace of his home in Hutchinson, Kansas, he has a nose bleed but he does not notice that. In fact, the boy does not seem to notice very much at all, he tells us in a soft voiceover that he has lost at least five hours of his life and that it is simply a blank in his memory. The last thing he remembers was sitting on the bench at his little league game, it started to rain, he looks to the sky and then zoom, it's all gone, nothing there and his mind is an empty slate. His mother, you would probably say is a tad overbearing and just a little smothering, his father is disappointed in his less than macho little son, who is not quite the tough little guy he wanted. In his bed little Brian has a dream, he is still in his baseball uniform, there is a blue background and some shadowy people appear in the shimmery distance. This is when the nightmares started, Brian tells us, again in an almost ominous voiceover giving it a slightly disconcerting impression on the senses. He wets the bed and has nosebleeds from here on and then there are the blackouts that also start to steal his time. Some little while later there is interference on the TV and it won't work properly, suddenly there are bright lights outside and off they trot, just in time to see what appears to be a UFO. Whether it is or not is, left deliberately unclear as this helps build the intrigue and mystery that surrounds this young boy. Does he really believe he was abducted by aliens during those lost five hours of his life, is that why he keeps having blackouts? Did they do experiments on him?

Our attention then gets pulled to the other central character of this dark tale, another young boy, Neil, he is looking through a window at home, watching his mother and her boyfriend have sex. For some reason he cannot wait to tell his baseball coach. Yes, he joined the little league team at the start of the summer and is already the star player, better than all the other kids, who to be fair are the greatest of players, little Brian seemingly is the worst. After a game, the coach declares the team is going out for a celebration, but when it comes down to it, there is just the coach and Neil, which is fine by Neil. There are dark sinister overtones to everything from here on and at times, you really feel your skin start to crawl. The ominous ever present sense of fear and danger encapsulate every single scene that features the coach. The coach's house is an Aladdin's cave of toys, treats and technology to boys of Neil's age, including, comics, games, massive TV's and junk food. The little kid thinks the coach is oh so cool. The coach takes some Polaroid photos and they seem to have a little fun, but it is clear this is just an act of grooming on the part of the coach.

After the next match the coach takes Neil to his house again and shows him the Polaroid photos in an album, they gorge themselves on snacks, and cereal before the coach starts to kiss the young boy.

There are many other aspects to the story of these two young lads, Neil seems to have learnt a great deal about the rudimentary, practical and physical aspects of sex, yet ultimately, not the real reasons to engage in it. It is disturbing and dark and as Neil grows and matures, he develops a passion for older men, but is this for affection and love or for what they can offer or pay him? Brian is convinced he was abducted by aliens and meets a girl who believes she was also taken by little green men and experimented on. When she wants to take her friendship with Brian a stage further, it confuse, disturbs and repulses him and he wants nothing further to do with the girl.

There is only one person who can now help Brian as we travel on a couple of years, his old little league baseball chum Neil, who is now living and working as a male hooker in New York. Brian finally gets the answer to the questions that have been haunting him since those lost five hours when he was eight.

A deeply heart wrenching film that bumps along with depth and darkness with great strength. You will almost certainly find yourself pulled into the story of the two lads and how their shared experience goes on to shape their adolescence and ultimately effect the rest of their lives. The film is very faithful to the novel and those with experience of the latter will recognise huge chunks of the narration throughout the action as the complete sorry tale unfolds.

There are stunning performances from the actors, especially Chase Ellison and George Webster who are without doubt exceptionally convincing and believable as the young Brian and Neil. This film could have fallen and the first hurdle had these two gifted kids not put in such a potently powerful performance, so they should be justly proud of their efforts.

The screenplay is based on the fictionalised autobiography by Scott Heim which in as equally moving, however this is not a movie to put on to make you feel good on a rainy Sunday afternoon, it's a movie to move you, make you really feel things, some emotions you might not want to feel. Intentionally dark and brooding this is a disturbing sensitive journey and you will discovery various tragically sad moments. However, there are lighter moments, amusing and funny, which may seem surprising given the subject matter. It sounds completely wrong to utter the phrase, I like a film about child abuse, yet I find Mysterious Skin to be a deeply moving, utterly compelling passionate dark movie and I cannot recommend it highly enough. Bold, daring, provocative even harrowing at times and one of the most affecting films concentrating on child abuse that has ever been produced. Yet is it influential? Many psychologists and therapists have praised its accurate and realistic portrayal of the long-term effects of child abuse and exploitation; regularly listed as one of the best gay films on the market.

"Mysterious Skin is not a happy film, no laugh a minute joy ride, it takes a difficult subject and expands on it with compassion, the end scene had me in tears and I hardly ever cry at things on the screen" **Adam, Cardiff.**

"An engrossing tale of child abuse and its life long lasting effects which really make you feel for the characters. One of the best films I have ever seen, especially considering what it is about. I don't know if it is influential or not, I just know it really gets under your skin" **Max, Salford.**

9

My Beautiful Laundrette

Director: Stephen Frears

Writer: Hanif Kureishi

Starring: Saeed Jaffrey, Roshan Seth, Gordon Warnecke Daniel Day-Lewis

Critically acclaimed, My Beautiful Laundrette is a true masterpiece of British cinema, a remarkable film detailing a collide of cultures, minds and values set against a backdrop of Thatcher's troubled and dysfunctional Britain. The incredible images, impressive camera work, superb cinematography combined with an epic screen play with intricately created dialogue of a highly charged and provocative story make this one of the greatest British films, not just of the eighties, but of all time. Directed by Stephen Frears and written by Hanif Kureishi, My Beautiful Laundrette took the world by storm in 1985/86 for its portrayal of gay love, homophobia, racism, capitalism and colliding cultures in such a vibrant and honest way. It was truly a landmark film and for any gay teenager growing up in the 80's a tour de force of hope and possibility. It seemed to come with such authentic honesty that many at the time believed it must have come from the mind of a gay man; however, Hanif Kureishi the writer was a heterosexual male with an incredible vision and remarkable ability.

Essentially this is the story of life, love and passion, Gordon Warnecke plays Omar, a bright young man who lives with his father in a rather squalid small flat overlooking the railway. His father, Hussein, a former famous Pakistani journalist is rather dissatisfied with Britain, its international politics and his life in general. It is this sense of dissatisfaction and disenfranchisement following a family tragedy that has led to his apparent alcoholism. Omar has had to become completely self-reliant and repeatedly is the sole caregiver to his father, which he does without complaint. Nasser, played by the incredible Saeed Jaffrey, is Omar's successful entrepreneur uncle and seems to be a very powerful and active member of London's close-knit Pakistani community. He is a man of wealth, with many contacts and his fingers are in a fair few pies. Omar takes a job with his uncle, at first it is only menial work such as washing cars at one of his uncle's garages, yet the young gentleman's work ethic is demonstrative to me strong. He wants to make something of his life, he wants achieve great things and after much cajoling and pleading his uncle finally sets him the task of turning a dilapidated, run down laundrette into a business with a future and turning a profit.

At times it feels that Nasser views Omar more as a son than a nephew and involves him in a great deal of social business activities at his house, meeting many family members like Tania, is Nasser's daughter. There is a spark between the two, although what that spark is, we are not quite sure, but Nasser seems to think he has found the future groom for his headstrong daughter at last. It is also at one of these gatherings that Omar meets another Pakistani businessman, Salim, yet not all of Salim's business interests are on the level. He is a bit of a shadowy figure that traffics illegal substances, he hires Omar to collect a shipment of drugs from the airport and deliver them. It is whilst Omar is driving Salim and his wife that evening that they are waylaid by a small group of thuggish racist youth. Among their number, Omar recognizes an old school friend, Johnny and they plan to rekindle their friendship.

Johnny, played to exception by the then relatively unknown Daniel Day Lewis, helps Omar transform the cruddy laundrette from a den of grime to a remarkable transcendental palace of cleanliness complete with aquarium and glitter balls. Needing more money for the transformation of the laundrette, Omar makes a risky move by flogging one of Salim's drug deliveries himself. Omar and Johnny are very close and it is whilst they transform the laundrette that we see the true nature of their relationship start to flourish and romance is heavy in the air.

Nasser makes a visit to the new laundrette on its grand opening, with his mistress, Rachel and whilst they dance in the front of the launderette, behind the big fish tank in the back Omar and Johnny are having sex. Tania also attends the opening where she confronts Rachel in a rather harsh way, causing her and Nasser to fight in the road, before storming off. Omar, whilst under the influence of alcohol proposes to Tania, who agrees and Omar's father also makes a brief appearance, he appeals to Johnny to convince Omar to head off to college, thinking it undignified for a son of his to run a launderette.

Omar takes on the management of another two laundrettes, owned by another contact of Nasser, with the help of Salim. Salim is driving Johnny and Omar to view one of the new laundrettes properties, when he sees the group of thugs that had previously abused him and his wife. Salim demonstrates his dislike of these British thugs by trying to run them down, racial tension mounts.

Tania drops by the laundrette to inform Johnny she's about to run away from home, outside the thugs are congregating, ready to pounce, but not on her, they are waiting for something, or someone. A little later Salim arrives and after he enters the laundrette, the aggrieved ruffians set about his car, he runs out and is ambushed. It could be a nasty attack, a violent beating; however, help is at hand in the shape of a reluctant Johnny. It is this action ensures Johnny is also beaten and bashed, but is saved by Omar. A few loose ends are tied but that essentially is the end of the film.

Described like this, it is perhaps hard to see why it was such an important and landmark film, yet it managed to encapsulate all the tensions of the economically troubled times with panache and tenacious realistic style. There are numerous aspects of importance at work here, not least the prejudicial racial tensions, demonstrated on both sides of the English / Asian divide, which were oh so common during those days of Thatcher's Britain. Homophobia ran rampant and unchallenged by authority indeed it was practised most by the Tory government and so homosexuality was also a key ingredient to this film along with the rather matter of fact way it was presented, which left little room for argument. There are also issues evolving around the merging of Asian ancestral behavioural and cultural loyalties with the British way of living, which often does not run smoothly. As this was originally a 'made for TV' movie it could quite easily have descended into soap opera and over sentimentality, yet it managed to stay way above that line, thankfully so. Also with comedic touches here and there it is prevented from falling into a possible gloomy pit of self-obsessed depression, again this is a fine testament to the skills of both the writer and director. My Beautiful Laundrette remains to this day a wonderful and remarkable piece of British cinema.

"'My beautiful launderette'. The Daniel Day Lewis character, Johnny, is not frightened by the haters, nor of loving Omar. The film exposes gay and racial hatred, in both the white and Asian communities, and shows gay people who are tough, and act honourably, with love and tenderness - in other words who don't act 'differently' from the way everybody else behaves. They are only different in their sexuality." **Alec, Cambridge.**

"Loved My Beautiful Laundrette - having a UK gay film is ace!" **Anne Brooke, Author, Surrey.**

"Part of my youth is in the film My Beautiful Laundrette, it transformed my life, gave me hope for the future that I could be accepted as a gay British Asian boy. It told me with hard work I could overcome the prejudices I experienced from both communities. Without this film I may not have had the

courage to be open about my sexuality, not at that time I did it. I would most probably have stayed in the closet for a few more years until I left home and perhaps missed out on a large part of life. To me, you can't get much more influential than that." **Azam, Middlesex.**

"An exceptional film, a real open window on life in England in the mid-eighties." **Martin, Falmouth.**

8

A Single Man

Director: Tom Ford.
Starring: Colin Firth, Julianne Moore, Nicholas Hoult, Matthew Goode.

Colin Firth heads a superb cast in this delightful motion picture drama based upon the sensitive poignant Christopher Isherwood novel 'A Single Man'. An exquisitely created cinematic debut from director Tom Ford that floats effortlessly along an agonisingly sorrowful tale of love, life and death.

Wonderfully shot in just three weeks this film is achingly beautiful film takes place on 30th November 1962 revolving around a day in the life of emotionally challenged English professor teaching at a Los Angeles college at a time of the Cuban missile crisis. The award winning Colin Firth takes up the lead role of George Falconer, a native Englishman, now residing under the Californian sun, who is finding the going a little tough. It has only been eight months since Jim, his beloved partner of sixteen years died in a terrible car accident. An event that still haunts George on a daily basis, even though he wasn't there at the time of the accident.

The only reason Jim and George were not together at the time of the crash was that Jim was on his way to visit his horribly homophobic and stuffy family. Colin Firth shows his true ability as master craftsman of this acting business in a tear-making scene back at the time of the accident when Jim's family inform him of the accident, death and the fact that he is not welcome at the funeral. Mr Firth plays such rapid flux of emotions from concern to shock, pain, anger and total obliteration with just his eyes and face as few others have the ability and skill to even attempt, let alone triumph. All the way through the film, there is a delicate and gentle narration from Firth as George, which provides tender insights highlighting the story. This day, 30th November is the day that George has will be the day he gets his affairs all together and in in order before he takes the ultimate step to be reunited with

Jim. His best friend, Charley calls, she is equally depressed but paints on a smile and a fake light-hearted attitude and frivolity.

George is clearly depressed, having never fully recovered from Jim's death, showers and dresses. He tells his cleaning lady Alva she has always been wonderful, George hugs her, which leaves her utterly confused, and off he goes, to work and attending to a few things, but before he leaves, he packs a gun in his briefcase. At college George gives a lecture about fear, minorities and acceptance, in which he also touches on recreational drug use, it is an unusually frank lecture. Student, Kenny Potter, played by Nicholas Hoult, yes he of the wonky mouth and pointy eyebrows fame that was the Boy in About A Boy and Tony in the first, and best, series of teen drama Skins. Loiters around to converse with George after class, he says he had never heard George express himself so openly in class, it is rather touching and intricate. Kenny buys George a pencil sharpener as a simple token of gratitude.

George returns to his car after clearing his office and collecting his gun, however he had not bargained for bumping into young Kenny again. Kenny has noticed the professor has cleared his office and seems depressed and invites him for a drink. The invitation from the young student is carefully declined with a gentle 'some other time' line as he already has plans with his friend Charley that evening. On the way back George calls into the bank, although it isn't a social visit, he collects all the important documents from his bank vault, when he sees a photo of Jim, his mind reminisces about a conversation with him on the beach.

George bumps into Carlos, a Hispanic hooker at the convenience store and they share a couple of drinks and some smokes together chatting away for a while before George heads on home. Another subtle delicate flashback occurs at the sound of a record and then in a strangely amusing scene George practices shooting positions for later on, he just cannot seem to get it right. However, time is pressing on and he's due at Charley's apartment, he does not really want to go, but he knows he must. Whilst there they talk and drink like old friends so, recollecting tales of London life, her ex-husband and so on. There is cutting tension when drink loosened lips suggest she and George could have had a "normal" life together if he had not been a "poof." It deeply offends George.

On the way home, George has a flashback to the time when he met Jim in a bar in 1946, just after the war. He decided to visit the very same bar again, now though, it is a quiet place, and he gets a scotch. Suddenly there is Kenny, the student from earlier, they chat and decide rather spontaneously to go to the beach and take a quick skinny dip.

Whilst at George's house, Kenny tells George he has a slight cut on the head and while the young lad attends to it, he notices a naked photo of Jim in the medicine's cabinet. George sees Kenny strip off his wet clothes, but does nothing about it; Kenny stays the night on the couch. In the early hours of the morning George awakes, he finds his gun under Kenny's covers; he takes it and puts it away, while the boy slumbers on. Then in the final piece of narration George tells us that he has rediscovered the ability to 'feel rather than think'.

Colin Firth won a BAFTA and a Copa Volpi for this role and it is easy to see why, he plays the role with tact, dignity and incredible feeling, I know he is renowned for playing upper crust English gentlemen, but in this role, he really excels. Julianne Moore is incredibly evocative as Charley; the drunken scene between the two is powerfully jolly whilst also remaining deeply affecting. Nicholas Hoult, who very nearly missed out on the role is incredibly impressive as student Kenny and all credit to him for stepping in just a few days before shooting began. Jamie Bell, the actor that played the young Billy Elliott had been cast on the role, but for some reason the insanely arrogant and unsavoury Bell failed to turn up to a costume fitting a few days before shoots, a potential disaster for the film, however, Tom Ford remembered Nicholas Hoult's audition and called him in. Thank god he did, for young Hoult made the role his own and was a million times better then Bell could ever have offered.

Matthew Goode is also jolly remarkable as the long lost Jim and is refreshingly enchantingly handsome whilst remaining slightly mystic mysterious and somehow affecting an 'other worldly' charm.

There is a brief little cameo appearance from Don Bachardy in one scene, Don was the long-time partner of Christopher Isherwood, and according to Tom Ford, was a great help during the writing of the screenplay. In the scene he's in, he wears Isherwood's lucky red socks!

It is a deeply moving drama, heavily accented with sorrow and depression, yet delicately light and compelling from start to finish. I am not always a fan of slipping into black and white to indicate the recollection of memories in movies, but when it is done well with tact and delicacy, it becomes acceptable. Such beautiful cinematography and intelligent scripting and interpretations helped ensure box office and critical success for this 2009 dramatic masterpiece of love and longing. The fact that this was Tom Ford's first outing as a director and he financed the entire film himself is incredible and amazing and he should be applauded and celebrated for creating something so utterly magical and compelling. The setting, sets, scenery, costumes and musical score are all wonderful aspects of a movie made with care, attention and I dare say a big dollop of love, so perfect are they all, either in isolation or together. I am trying to find fault with this film, but such a task is proving difficult, I will settle with the fact that it was not long enough and for me could have been eked out another ten minutes or so! Seriously, it is a faultless movie and whilst the influence it offers is still relatively limited due to its recent nature, I am sure it will be felt for years to come. It achieved an impressive total of £16 million approximately at the box office. I would also add that maybe this has set a bar in terms of quality that other serious mid-budget films will forever onward have to match to be considered truly great.

"Colin Firth got a BAFTA for best actor for his role in A Single Man and this is rightly deserved, he is absolutely stunning and this is a highlight of his career. He acts so incredibly well in it that he should also have got an OSCAR for it. The whole film is magnificent, I close my eyes and I see the faces of the two characters, I feel them in my heart and in my mind." **Anon.**

"Everything about A Single Man is extraordinary, this is how movies are supposed to be. Perfection." **Maggie, London.**

"How emotive the loss of ones lover and ones self. A Single Man is a magnificent film working many levels around grief and love. Firth is outstanding and Nick Hoult is a star of the future, the camera loves him and thousands of new fans do now, of that there can be no doubt. It moved me to tears at the festival, where we applauded until our hands threatened to fall off. It continues to move me to tears. **Richard, Brighton.**

7

Torch Song Trilogy

Director: Paul Bogart.

Starring: Harvey Fierstein, Anne Bancroft, Matthew Broderick, Brian Kerwin, Eddie Castrodad, Ken Page, Charles Pierce.

Harvey Fierstein started performing as a drag artist in Manhattan clubs from the age of 15; even before that age he knew he was just a bit different. He became widely known on the New York club circuit and was more often than not to be found playing drag roles in off off Broadway shows. Following a bad break-up Harvey set about writing a play detailing the difficult and painful experience, this became the play 'The International Stud' and was presented in New York during 1976. The play introduced the character of Arnold Beckoff to the world, writing a further two semi-autobiographical plays about Arnold's life. Eventually Harvey conjoined and amalgamated these three plays into just one, 'Torch Song Trilogy' which, had its stage debut off off Broadway in 1981, where it ran for almost 1230 performances.

Torch Song Trilogy was adapted from stage for cinema and came out in 1998, directed by Paul Bogart and not surprisingly starring Harvey as Arnold Beckoff. Also included in the cast were Brian Kerwin, sexy stunner Matthew Broderick, screen legend Anne Bancroft and infamous American female impersonator Charles Pierce.

The play version ran for over four hours, something not possible in film and thus many cuts, exclusions and edits had to be employed to bring it down to a studio demanded running time of two hours. Without wishing to ignore the onset of AIDS whilst also not wishing to alter the entire fabric of the story the timeline of the movie was shifted back several years, started in 1971.

The story opens with a wonderfully amusing little set of linking scenes highlighting Arnold's rather unique childhood tastes. Then we shift to early 1971, Arnold is a female impersonator, working in a low down New York drag club, and the opening monologue he delivers in the mirror of the dressing room is simply a work of genius, a real magnum opus and sets the deeply personal tone for the whole move. Arnold accompanies friend and fellow drag queen Murray to a New York dive bar called the Stud and it's there then the seemingly shy Arnold meets Ed, a bisexual schoolteacher whose odd chat up lines include the "Your voice is really sexy, anyone ever tell you that" that could work you know, then follows it up with "Is that natural or do you have a cold?" which doesn't!

Arnold falls head over heels for Ed and whilst it is not exactly one sided, the balance is uneven; a situation not helped by Ed's bisexuality and general uncomfortable nature he has with matters of sexuality. He continues to date women, which comes as a surprise to Arnold at a spontaneous impromptu visit to Ed's apartment, they break up and it is tears before bedtime, or in this case before act one is put to bed!

An unlikely visitor to the club where Arnold is one of a team of drag entertainers come in the shape of handsome male model, Alan, played by the sweet and adorable Matthew Broderick, who I have to say has never looked better of more appealing than in he does in this movie. Rather surprisingly, they hit it off and we're walking down the road to happy ever after. They seem perfect together, sweet, loving, giving, honest and oh so romantic. Ed meanwhile marries the girl – Laurel, whom Arnold met so briefly at Ed's apartment and through a move worthy of a Coward play, Laurel invites Arnold and Alan up for the weekend.

Oh, there are some magical scenes played out during the weekend, not least an amusing battle of the bedsprings! Things happen and a roll in the hay is the route to a wonderful cinematic multi reaction edit, which still makes me smile. Relationships on both sides are tested and emerge strong and more cohesive. Life gets even better for Arnold and Alan when word comes through that they've been successful with their application and pretty soon a giant stork is going to come knocking at their door with a fifteen year old bundle of joy. Yep, they are getting the opportunity to foster the child, with a view to adoption and so they move to a bigger apartment. Sadly however, the neighbourhood is not one of the more enlightened and socially accepting ones, Alan, ever the courageous chivalrous young man runs to assist an old victim of a brutal homophobic gay bashing by the local street gang. It is rather horrific, powerfully played out and emotionally charged.

The third and final act starts off some time in or around spring of 1980, Arnold's mother, Ma, played by the wonderful Anne Bancroft, is coming for a quick visit all the way from Florida where she moved to after her husband died, because it's what 'they' do. There is a major misunderstanding at the bust stop when she first meets David, the foster son, she thinks he is a mugger at first, a mugger in a suit, but a mugger nonetheless. Its quickly resolved when David informs her he is Arnold's foster son, a fact that Arnold himself had neglected to mention. She does not approve, she does not understand, she thinks Arnold has already turned David gay, it all comes out in a vibrant angry and dramatic argument sequence that demonstrates how talented these two wonderful performers are. It is not just the one argument either, there are a few of them, each powerful, each well scripted with some gems of lines batted back and forth.

On a side line, Ed who is temporarily staying with Arnold as his marriage ends, confesses he has grown up, matured and is much more sure of himself, his sexuality and more importantly what he wants – which is the life he has with Arnold. Somehow, love conquers all and no matter how unlikely, they bury the hatchet, thankfully not in each other's heads, before she head on back to Florida, finally it seems she accepts him for who he is and Arnold has pretty much everything he is ever wanted.

It is a deeply affecting film, emotional and funny to the extreme and yet it works marvellously well, which I am sure is thanks mainly to the authentic way Harvey tells it as Arnold. There are such wonderful moments, high drama, deep sadness and almost unbridled joy, that watching Torch Song Trilogy could be considered of riding on a roller coaster of emotions. However, that should be seen as and is indeed a good thing; it allows you scope to feel things that perhaps you had not even noticed in yourself, or others. It gives you the power to see the good and bad in the characters of others, in all our Technicolor differences. The cast are superb; Anne Bancroft is without hesitation extraordinary as Ma, demonstrating her ability as a great actress in fine style. Hat's off to both Matthew Broderick and Brian Kerwin who play the two love interests, both touching and believable. Eddie Castrodad does a fine job as the young man David, who we all wanted to adopt; at least he could do his own dusting, although the diet Pepsi on cereal at breakfast time was a bit hard to stomach. The script is pure comic class, heavy on both gags and sentiment from the very opening to the time the credits start to roll at the end. Harvey Fierstein is superb in the role as Arnold, but that should not come as much of a surprise considering he wrote the piece and in part it is semi-autobiographical. So many of the lines have slipped from the movie into generalised social commentary of dozens and dozens of gay men of a certain age. "Nobody comes that way!" "I am upset, I am uptight, I am up to my nipples in Southern Comfort and you want to take advantage of me. Fine" "A problem is never as permanent as a solution" "A, I want children and B, if anyone asks, I am the pretty one!" "You cheated me out of your life and then blamed me for not being there!" I could go on and on, however these are just some I can remember off the top of my head. Torch Song Trilogy had some powerful messages to heave into the collective consciousness of the audience, and in some ways, it was way ahead of his time. If influence were just about box office receipts alone then Torch Song Trilogy would be toward the mid-point of the listing, amassing around £3 million worldwide. Thankfully, influence goes way beyond just the take at the box office, or hardly any of the lower budget films, with limited cinema releases or access would have made the top 50. Besides, it did so so much better in video and DVD sales. Movies can really move and shape people's lives, changing emotions, situations and ideals, Torch Song Trilogy is one of those movies, a powerful piece of comic drama, that due to its subject and its audience did much better on video and DVD than in movie theatres.

"I commend late eighties film Torch Song Trilogy to your compilation of top influential movies. This New Line cinema film details the trials and tribulations of human relations set within the colourful life of a New York drag artiste. Written for the stage, adapted for the screen and starring Harvey Fierstein this the finest example of gay filmmaking and I cannot recommend it highly enough." **Gregory, St Louis.**

"Torch Song Trilogy, is a super touching moving tale of family relationships within the gay community. Greatly funny in places and horribly heartbreaking in others, it really helps you understand how life is not always easy for gay people, who on the surface look like that have such happy lives." **Sally, Newcastle.**

"Harvey Fierstein is an amazing as drag queen Arnold in Torch Song Trilogy, he has a voice so low and grating it is hard to imagine him pretending to be a woman, till you hear him sing! He carries the whole film, which like the play, was a social documentary of not just being gay in New York in a world before AIDS, but what it was like to be a happy positive gay man. It came out at a time when positive role models for gay men were few and far between. It showed that life could really get better, there was hope for happiness, even after great adversity." **Drew, Cambridge.**

"From the very opening scenes Torch Song Trilogy takes us on a tour of thoughts, feelings, experiences that most of us gay men have been on or have some knowledge of. Of course these are exaggerated for dramatic effect but that makes them no less important. The pace and settings were tremendously good, the horrific gay bashing was disturbing, the dysfunctional relationship with the mother was perfectly balanced, the desire to adopt a little explored aspect of gay relations in cinema, and that tremendous script.This movie is second to none." **John, Queensland.**

"I got this on VHS with my 16th Birthday money, I had to keep it secret along with my sexuality. I watched it over and over and over again and each time I cried with laughter and I cried with sadness. I cried for everything it shows that I couldn't have, I laughed at every joke, even the ones I didn't get till much later. I still have that old VHS, even though it doesn't play anymore, because I doubt I would have got through my teenage years without it." **Simon, Newcastle.**

"Torch Song Trillogy, is my suggestion for the most influential film, it is from 88. Just one line – 'There's one more thing you better understand, I've taught myself to sew, cook, fix plumbing, build furniture – I can even pat myself on the back when necessary. All so I don't need to ask anyone for anything. There is nothing I need from anyone except for love and respect and anyone who cant give me those two things has no place in my life' need I say any more?" **Dennis, Dorset.**

6

Beautiful Thing.

Director: Hettie Macdonald

Starring: Glen Berry, Linda Henry, Meera Syal, Ben Daniels, Scott Neal, Tameka Empson

There are some films you watch and whilst you may enjoy them at the time you know you'll forget about that as soon as the end credits roll, then there are those films that manage to stay in your mind for a day or two. However, then there are those extraordinarily rare outstanding films that you know will stay with you for the rest of your life, Beautiful Thing is one of the latter. A wonderfully expressive coming of age drama about two schoolboys finding love set against the harsh grey concrete jungle of a Thamesmead council estate.

Introspective Jamie is a quite misunderstood boy, his mother Sandra, is a rather brash, no-nonsense, tough talking woman with a heart of gold and typical of the inhabitants of a slightly run down London council estate. She works as a barmaid in a local pub but holds aspirational desires to manager a pub of her own away from the grime of gritty and claustrophobic Thamesmead estate. A few doors down is the adorable Ste, a keen football playing sports loving lad, whose warm smile hides some dark secrets. Next-door to Sandra and Jamie lives the adorable former school mate Leah and her mother. Leah has a thing for old music such as the Mama's and the Papa's as well as Ste's older brother, local wide boy, Trevor.

Trevor deals drugs and just like his father is handy with his fists, burning the tea one afternoon seems to warrant a beating for young Ste. Sandra takes pity on the young teenager and offers him refuse at he's although he will have to top 'n' tail with Jamie. There is wonderful closeness between the boys, some tender exchanges as they both open themselves as feelings of more than just friendship seems to grow between them.

Ste is their houseguest for a second night, only this time, the two lads do not top and tail; there is some awkward conversation, some tender words and even the very first kiss. It is amazingly tender and gentle. In the morning, Ste is a little spooked, embarrassed and perhaps even a little in denial regarding what took place during the night and makes his leave before Jamie awakes.

He then avoids Jamie for some days, refusing to come to terms with his sexuality and his burgeoning feelings for his schoolmate and neighbour.

In a highly authentic scene, the shy and sensitive Jamie eventually plucks up courage to steal a copy of Gay Times, the UK's only month gay magazine at the time the film is set. In the safety and privacy of his room, he read the glossy from cover to cover, his eyes and his mind wide open. For any confused and emotionally conflicted teen, it is a revelation, he is not alone in the world, and there are others and a surprising number of gay bars, pubs and clubs to go to, including one a short bus ride from the Thamesmead estate.

Jamie and Ste finally come together in the back garden of a house party, words are exchanged as they face up to each other's sexuality, and it is an interesting and touching moment. The party does not end well, first of all there is a vicious scene between Sandra and Leah, a payback for Leah's meddling gossip and lies. Moreover, in an effort to score some of Trevor's drugs cheap off Ste Leah lets slip that she knows the boys did not top and tail on the second night, she covered for him in front of Ste's alcoholic father and abusive brother. This scares the hell out of Ste, already consumed with confusion over his emotions and feelings for Jamie, he does a runner, into the dark night on the estate.

The beautifully shot film expands over the hard angular and often deemed ugly surroundings of a real life concrete jungle with such finesse it makes it appear almost graceful and attractive and a place you would want to be. I wonder how often that can be said of inner London concrete cramped council estates.   However because the story is so passionate and interesting, the acting of the central cast so incredibly solid and believable it's often becomes difficult to ascertain, accept and acknowledge the stark beauty of the surroundings.

There is an exceptional scene where Sandra jumps in a black cab shouting 'follow that bus' after her son and Ste jump aboard a the red double decker, she follows them to The Gloucester, a gay pub, and her pinched lips scowling face take us on a whirlwind fast range of emotions it is positively breath taking. The pub scene itself is also so believable, not least for it's seemingly clique atmosphere of regulars but also the impressive performance by drag queen extraordinaire Dave Lynn.   There is fear, shyness; amusement, wonderment and pride showing on the two lads faces during just the few seconds on screen that mirror the exact feelings of countless thousands of teenage gay boys heading into a gay pub for the very first time. Following this is an exceptionally romantic and exquisite staged run and chase through a moonlit park, tender moments, stolen glances, giggles, laughter and a kiss takes the 'ahh' factor to notch number ten. Love really is alive, well, and living in an inner city park at the dead of night.

The power and depth of the relationship between Jamie and his mother Sandra is extoled in magnitude in a coming out / confrontation scene in their flat that could so easily have appeared stilted and fake, yet through the magic of Hettie MacDonald's direction, works like a dream. It is potent, powerful, laced with venom and tenderness, but above all, honesty. For me, it is a scene that is incredibly hard to forget, not that I would want to anyway.

Leah creates an amazing scene in a drug fuelled hallucination believes she has been reincarnated at Mama Cass and a hilarious scene follows of her walking on the balcony railings, wondering all over the manor and having to be rescued and cared for by Tony, Sandra's hippylike University Challenge watching younger boyfriend. It was a wonderful aspect of the film, which ensures that emotions don't fall down the sentimentality trap.

I adore the subplot of Sandra going for an interview with the brewery to become the manager and licensee of her own pub, which leads on to a pure magical and poignant scene of viewing the property, some many miles from the Thamesmead estate. The musical score at this particular juncture of the movie is damn near poetic perfection.

The remarkable end scene of the movie is a triumph and always leaves me with a tear or two, never before has dancing on the street seemed brave yet completely naturally wonderful. The two boys dancing together, Sandra and Leah uniting in an easy truce to dance alongside watched by a load of the other inhabitants of the estate is moving beyond words and way more that you first expect it to be. Yes there are indications of the stirrings of a lesbian affair, real or imagined, although added to the slightly lingering look Sandra earlier gave her barmaid and dance watching friend, I would not have been surprised. Perhaps that's why Sandra ended her relationship with Tony, dumping him along with the rubbish down the garbage chute!

There are a multitude of reasons why this particular film is so popular, so highly thought of and indeed so influential, not least the stunning performances by all the cast. I have tried incredulously hard to find a single fault with the acting, but that is a task I am happy to say I have failed at. Scott Neal and Glenn Berry are simply superb as Ste and Jamie and convey the whole plethora of emotions with accuracy and such authenticity. Linda Henry is utterly amazing as Sandra that mere words cannot adequately describe her performance, so uniquely exceptional as it was. Tameka Empson is so delightful as Leah and the lovely Ben Daniels is outstanding in the supporting role of Tony.

Beautiful Thing is a feel good movie as well as an honest account of coming to terms with sexual identities and first love. It is both poignant and funny in equal measure and pretty much guarantees moist eyes on every viewing. There may well be some that say it is unrealistic and fault the film for those, however, as we all know, sometimes-real life is more unrealistic than the movies! British movie excellence, need I really say more?

"Brilliantly acted, great storyline, real settings, deep meanings – beautiful thing is film perfection."

Andy, London.

"Beautiful Thing is a beautiful film, from start to finish, it has everything and more you could possibly want in a gay movie. A beautiful story of first love and growing up." **Karen, Manchester.**

"A Beautiful Thing seemed so real and what is was like growing up." **Anon**

"The influence is a personal thing and will depend on age. For me it was Beautiful Thing. It made me smile, a small tear as well and helped me. Though I doubt two gay teens dancing in a rough housing estate may not be welcomed with open arms by everyone!" **Stephen Chapman, Blogger, London.**

"The first gay film I saw that made me happy to be gay. It is pure joy and the end scene has you sobbing with happiness." **Jason King, Film Critic, Sydney.**

5

Shortbus

Director: John Cameron Mitchell

Starrring: Sook-Yin Lee, Paul Dawson, Lindsay Beamish, PJ DeBoy, Raphael Barker, Peter Stickles, Jay Brannan, Justin Bond.

Shortbus the 2006 American sexually charged comedic drama shocked and delighted audiences around the world, it has since gone down in history as one of the most sexually explicit films ever to be granted a general distribution certificate by film boards around the world. There is no skirting the issue, this is an explicit movie, it has full on sex which is as real as the bodily fluids that get spurted on faces and bodies, although not pictures. However, before you jump to the conclusion this is just hard-core porn by another name, be aware that it was written and directed by respected filmmaker John Cameron Mitchel, him from Hedwig fame and it transcends normal sexually explicitness with a deeply affecting storyline and a journey of self-discovery.

It achieved a worldwide box office total or around $5.5 million, although DVD sales have way more than matched that, it also went to win many awards at various festivals all over the world and was critically acclaimed, at least in the most part. It certainly has gained a fair slice of publicity for the many actors in the film, not least the lovely Jay Brannan, who plays Ceth and has a song on the soundtrack, the deceptively deep SodaShop. His infectious smile, simpering nervous giggle and delicate voice hint at a vulnerability that makes everyone want to look after him, before or after they shag him senseless.

John Cameron Mitchell bases the plot around an endearing sex therapist/couples counsellor Sofia Lin in New York City, she is married to the dishy but dim Rob who has amazingly potent and dextrous contortionist sex, yet there is a problem. One of the couples seeking counselling she encounters is James, allegedly a former rent boy and Jamie a former child actor, they need to communicate more, however in the common cruel twist of therapy it is the clients that come to help the therapist. She confides in them that although she is a sex, sorry couple's therapist, she is pre-orgasmic; meaning she's never had an orgasm, not ever! To help her hunt for the big O, they invited her to the freakishly good underground sexually expressive artistic boutique like salon they go to called Shortbus!

The host of Shortbus, the club is an infamous New York entertainer, Justin Bond, who helps Sofia open her eyes and her mind to all the new experiences around her, of which there are plenty. Not least of all a mass orgy scene of writing naked bodies engaging in all manner couplings and sexual expressions, even the director is somewhere in the melee of human flesh on display. She strikes up a friendship with a dominatrix whore by the name Severin, who we saw earlier in a side scene whipping her client to surprising and incredibly far reaching conclusion.

One of the guests at the salon is a young handsome model come singer by the name of Ceth, who is seen using a handheld device to find a suitable mate, gosh sounds so familiar to these days when gay guys about town are switching on their mobile smart phones and turning to Grindr! What's the about art imitating life? Anyway, that flunks out and he meets James and Jamie and jingle jangle sparks fly and we have ourselves a funky threesome of fine fanciable fellas.

All this is closely watched by a stalker kind of character, which does not quite make a whole ton of sense, but then this is the movies and anything can happen, although on the DVD you will find excess deleted scenes which exemplify this character with an even more implausible line of story as an assistant to the US President. The hard on three-way sex scene between Jamie, James and Ceth is one of the best and one of the funniest sexual explorations I have ever seen in a film of this sort. It is erotic, exotic, sexy yet also strangely empowering and thus works on many levels and I wonder how many people have since gone on to use a penis as a microphone and sung a national anthem into such a place? I don't know about you, but I think I noticed a few bum notes!

Sofia and Severin spend more and more time together, deep meaningful conversations help the sex therapist to confront her tightness regarding sexual matters. Severin also starts to develop and understand her own desires, wishes and needs. However we find out the James has secretly been documenting his life in video a living visual biography and suicide note. The final scene of course is his own death, so he tried to drown himself in the swimming pool with a plastic bag on his head. It is rather dramatic, scary even and thank god, for a stalker is all I can say, because, that is who comes to the rescue, his very own stalker. Phew!

There are several more scenes were each of the characters confront their feelings, exploring their inadequacies and their desires, some obvious and some less so. Each one has various problems or obstacles to overcome on the way to enlightenment and ultimate happiness, which is to be honest the way we are erotically heading. It all comes together, if you'll pardon the pun, at the final orgy scene, Jamie and James, Ceth and the stalker, Severin takes control of Rob, Sofia joins a sexy couple which leads her to passionately embrace her first orgasm. The worlds wrongs are righted, at least that is the feeling expressed as the film ends with an emotive song sung by Justin Bond.

Shotbus is one hell of a ride, that much is for sure, and John Cameron Mitchell is a formidable director who employs a theatrical sense to a lot of the action and the atmosphere evoked with the Shotbus club is a triumph. It is an exuberant exploration of sexualities and sex which is evident from the very opening to the very ending and you know, it is not ashamed of it, nor does it exploit the realness of it all. There have been other films that have used hard-core real authentic sex to tell a story, 9 songs for example, to push the boundaries, but unlike 9 songs, there really is a story between the sex scenes in Shortbus and you really do develop a bond and care for the characters by the end. It is not an action film as such, although there is a lot of 'action' in it, it is more an emotion extravaganza and as such, there are a couple of slower and quieter moments. Whilst these aren't boring, they do inter-splice the telling of our lead characters advancements and accomplishments, at worst allow you to make a brew without pressing pause and best make you accept that the girls have a point.

It has an interesting and charming cast, from sad song singer Jay Brannan as the delightfully giggly Ceth, to PJ DeBoy and Paul Dawson as Jamie and James. I adored Canadian radio star Sook-Yin Lee as Sofia Lin who excels at this role and performs with such understated passion and honesty that I was practically feeling her orgasm with her. Raphael Barker is the cheeky straight boy next door, the jock with a heart, Rob and is interesting to watch. Peter Stickles is exemplary as the stalker character and I feel almost betrayed that the bizarre deleted scenes were not in the final cut of the movie, such is the ability of that actor. Justin Bond should be credited for a fine performance, how I would love to have him at my next garden party. A small, but nonetheless significant role was that of the former New York mayor, played by Alan Mandell, who spoke so eloquently and for older gay folk everywhere with aplomb.

There was some discussion when I mentioned including this film in the countdown, 'but it's not a gay film' I was challenged, which is true, I'll readily admit that Shortbus is most defiantly not exclusively a gay film, in so much that it has straight folk doing straight folk things in it. However, many people suggested it during the research, and well over half of all onscreen time and action involves and surrounds the lives of the gay characters. Shortbus is not defined with finely drawn lines, this is about homosexuality and this bit is about heterosexuality, in entirety it is all about sexuality as a great big whole. It is more than a little audacious in that respect but powerfully and rightly so. Through the scenes, we explore virtually every avenue that there is to go down, explore, enjoy or send a postcard from. I hate to use the phrase, there is something here for everyone, but from speaking to loads of different people, we all took something different from this movie, which ultimately is a powerful indication of influential filmmaking.

"I love 'Shortbus' because it meant a lot to me sexually, and the desperate attempts to connect seemed so real. Also because I fell in love with Jay Brannan and haven't got over him yet." **Alec, Cambridge.**

"I just ought to endorse Alec's support of 'Shortbus' Loved it!" **Ray, Worthing.**

"It has to be Shortbus, not only for the incredible in your face sex but also for its story. I loved it from start to finish." **Ben, Milan.**

"Shortbus moved me in ways no other movie had done before, or has done since." **Anon.**

4

The Birdcage

Director: Mike Nichols

Starring: Robin Williams, Nathan Lane, Gene Hackman, Christine Baranski, Dan Futterman, Calista Flockhart.

Put simply this is a glitzy, colourful, modern remake of La Cage aux Folles in which Robin Williams stars as the hairy and sweaty Armand, South Beach drag club owner alongside the incomparable Nathan Lane as the star and Armund's lover and partner Albert.

Just like the original version, their lives are turned upside down and inside out when Armund's son, Val, comes home to announce he is getting married to an ultra-conservative senator's daughter called Barbara. Everything goes haywire and speeds up to comic high gear when those future in-laws come down to meet their daughters intended and his family. Scandal is what the senator wants to avoid at the great cost, you cannot blame him, and his co-founder of the coalition for moral order partnership has just been found dead in the bed of an underage black prostitute.

There are laughs a plenty when first Armund and then Albert try and play it butch, they desperately need a woman and it's so not often you hear a couple of middle aged gay men scream that! In steps the wonderful and delightful Christine Baranski who always lights up the screen with a presence that is electrifying. However, is life that simple, that easy? You bet your sweet little arse it aint!

Barbara tells her parents that Armand is a cultural attaché to Greece, whilst Albert is a housewife, and that they divide their time between Greece and Florida. It is only a little white lie really, just as changing their last name from Goldman to Coleman is. The evening of the meeting arrives, the apartment above the drag club is transformed from gay paradise to near austere monastery, Val's real mother, Katherine (Baranski) is held up by traffic and a boat and out pops Albert as a wonderful creation of freakishly good yet awfully bad middle-aged mother. Armand and Val are both horrified at first but have no option to go along with the façade, which for some bizarre reason in this movie world works. More jokes, no proper meal and the most amazing china dinner service of naked boys playing leap- frog and still the senator and his wife do not catch on. Until that is at the door arrives

Katherine, introducing herself as Val's mother and the whole charade is shot to pieces, just as TV news crews arrive out front

How on earth can the senator and his wife leave the drag club without some kind of mass scandal erupting and ending his political career? The answer is simple, drag up and we are treated to the wonderful scene of Gene Hackman in a dress making the late great Bea Arthur look as feminine as a virginal princess.

It is a great feel good movie, full of lightness, the jokes and funny situation fire by in rapid succession that you will probably not catch them all on the first viewing. Robin William's is superb as the nightclub owner even if he does sweat profusely at times and almost cracks up completely in the kitchen scene with the houseman come butler. I adore Nathan Lane, with his scene stealing 'Starina' performance and utter camp flamboyant majesty. Gene Hackman is equally good as the chocolate addicted extreme right wing senator with his sour face and dry delivery.

As a modern re-make of a seventies classic it is both successful and complimentary, it also stands up on its own, which is a jolly good job, and for I am sure, the vast majority of its audience would not have seen La Cage aux Folles. Sure, it is lightweight, sure, it plays a little to stereotype, but it goes beyond them, reaching in to the human side and honest inner core aspect admirably. It is outrageously camp, unashamedly so, blatantly exotic and wonderfully charming, a great feel good movie.

Influential? Well, I suppose it must have done something right, it is to date the most grossing gay movie at the cinema of all time, the approximate box office takings amounted to more than £117 million. DVD sales topped charts around the world and you will find numerous 'The Birdcage' pubs and clubs all over this globe of ours, almost all without exception, gay or gay friendly venues that drew inspiration from the movie.

"The Birdcage is simply one of the best gay movies ever made, it is over the top, it is stereotypical, it is over acted because it is supposed to be. The drag side of the film is clearly meant to be stereotypical, it is written in that way, just like the original, yet it goes beyond those to expose real human emotions and also says, hey, don't take everything so seriously. There are so many gags running through The Birdcage, from start to finish, from steaks falling on the floor, muffs with tails, to big dicked statues in the desk by and a dog called piranha! It is simply hilarious" **Max, Weston Super Mere.**

"A brilliantly funny film with a prefect cast and great sets, it isn't meant to be a Philadelphia or a Schindlers list, its meant to be an entertaining and funny film, it succeeds hands down." **Amy, Brighton.**

3

The Adventures of Priscilla – Queen Of The Desert.

Director: Stephan Elliott

Starring: Hugo Weaving, Guy Pearce, Terence Stamp, Bill Hunter.

A relatively low budget Australian film about drag queens took the world by storm, almost caused a riot at the Cannes film festival and drove a million young queens to the dressing up box in the hunt for sequins, sparkles and pink flip-flops!

The Adventures of Priscilla, Queen of The Desert gave us such classic lines as, "Just what this country needs, another cock in a frock on a rock!" and "Listen here you mullet, why don't you just light your tampon and blow your box apart, it's the only bang you're ever going to get, sweetheart"

It is without exception the best and arguably the most successful drag queen movie of all time, breaking box office records and capturing the top of the charts in numerous countries around the world. It was an Academy award winning extravaganza of glitter, glam and lip-syncing with the most outrageously camp costumes the world had seen outside Madame JoJo's or Funny Girls! Uproariously funny and yet deeply affecting it proved to be way more than just a camp outing of tried and tested queer humour.

For those of you that don't know, of which there honestly can't be many, 'Priscilla' is at its very heart in the most simplistic terms, a classic road movie, yet it takes on many guises as we carry on down the highway of enlightenment, with a few pit stops along the way, essentially to camp it up with the locals. Two drag queens and a tranny come together in a bargain budget Barbie camper and head off up the road through the outback to a hot date in Alice Springs.

We follow the trials and trials of Mitzi Del Bra (Hugo Weaving) Felicia Jollygoodfellow (Guy Pearce) and Bernadette Bassenger (Terrance Stamp) as they escape the dodgy drag scene of Sydney in a big old bus and head off for a series of shows at a hotel and casino in the lovely yet dusty Alice Springs, right in the heart of the dead centre of Australia. They all have their own reasons to get away from it all for a while, Mitzi owes a favour, Felicia will do anything for a good time and transsexual Bernadette is getting over the death of her last boyfriend, who died peroxiding his hair in the bathroom!

Now, Alice Springs is a long long way from Sydney, which affords plenty of time for fabulous conversations, funny occurrences and outrageous mishaps.

aughing so much that tears fall down my face.its hilarious the things that happen in it are great. the costumes are amazing and the acting is great they really did a good job. i swear that if you hear the opening song that you will sing it sometime without knowing it.

The late eighties was a bit of a coming of age time for Australia's gay population, especially Sydney, it really came alive and blossomed into one of the bigger gay populations in the world. Australia has a reputation for all the big butch manly men, which considering how the modern nation of Australia started, would seem pretty accurate, only it's not, it's completely different, ever so much more vibrant and colourful. It is that vibrancy, that colour and that hopefulness that is so perfectly depicted in Priscilla.

Stephen Elliott, the director and writer, who incidentally has a small cameo in the movie as a cute door boy in Alice, says he saw drag shows in other places, like the US and England, which were essentially men in dresses lip-syncing to other peoples songs. In Australia they did the same, but took it in a completely new direction, it became a completely new strange variety of theatre, so much so that he even used to go to drag queen jelly wrestling, pushing the envelope to the maximum. It was this experience along with watching a drunken drag queen at the Sydney gay Mardi Gras, which gave birth to the movie idea, which took hardly any time at all to write.

From the very opening you know this film has deep rooted soul, first shots of Hugo as Mitzi mouthing the words to the poignant Charlene song, 'I've been to paradise, but I've never been to me' give the impression of an emotively sad song, yet this is so rapidly defused by the appearance of a lethargic priest and Felicia nursing a baby rubber chicken. You have left in no doubt after that that is no ordinary Australian movie and the jokes and gags just tumble on from there in rapid succession.

The rapid cuts of scenes depicting the start of this mega journey to the centre of Australia is so potently put together, you'd think it was several hours, yet is under five hours and the conversations make you laugh out loud, regardless of who you're with or the setting in which you are viewing this masterpiece of cinematic joy. Scene after scene after scene are perfectly played and incredibly funny with just a touch of real emotion. The ride is on, the further along the more we learn about our three super stars of sequins, Mitiz's got a wife, the person he owes the favour to, Felicia had a little set to with a pervy uncle when he was a small boy and Bernie's real name is Ralph!

Walking the main drag of a town called Broken Hill in drag is a true wonder and spectacle and I can only wonder at the reaction they really had from the locals. Oh and I am told the hotel with the tackiest of interiors in the world is a real place, can you imagine actually waking up to that? Following that is a classic scene in the working man's type bar where the immortal line 'listen here you mullet, why don't you light your tampon and blow your box apart, because it's the only bang you're ever going to get, sweetheart' is delivered with pure passion by Terrance in reply to, "No, you can't have, you can't have nothing, we've got nothing here for people like you, nothing." Its key scenes like this, packed with humour and emotion that take this film right to the hearts of the audience.

Seeing the graffiti sprayed on the side of the bus in pink paint the morning after shocks the trio along with the audience and strikes a chord with those of old enough to have lived through a time of such prejudice and discrimination and how true those word seem when they ring in our ears, that no matter how tough we think we are, such things still hurt.

Taking wrong turns and the bus breaking down is par for the course for a road movie and Priscilla does not disappoint in that score. Of course, they actually did the same during the film of the flick, so you know it has a scene of authenticity to it. It also allows us to have a remarkable feel good moment of the three stars dragging up during at outdoor party with the local aboriginal population. It is extraordinarily funny, amusing and beautifully shot and has pretty much everyone singing 'I will Survive' and you know, you can make a fine living in a pair of heels!

Abba fans may not have liked the whole Abba turd scene or the alleged Abba abuse the film supposedly dishes out to the former seventies super group. But apart from those and a few religious nutcases, Priscilla proved to be a massive hit with pretty much every audience brave enough to go and see it. There are deeply moving scenes, such as the gay bashing of Felicia and the confrontation between Mitzi and his son in Alice, which really seem seep through the comedy to dance in your heart and make you fall in love with the film.

One of the key aspects of the movie is the superb casting; Terrence Stamp previously typecast as your typical British villain, took a risk on the role of Bernadette and knocked it out of the water in a downbeat, down trodden put upon yet completely resilient way. Hugo Weaving is the less visually striking member of the trio and the central character of Mitzi, who really is the lynch pin between the two worlds. The role of Felecia is taken by the simply stunning Guy Pearce who had literally just left long running soap Neighbours, in which he played goodie two shoes Mike and was an inspired choice and oh so pretty. Guy's superb performance takes the movie to new heights and is so good that the he has had trouble-convincing people he is actually straight in real life, even to this day. Bill Hunter a massive Australian character actor shines outstandingly as the gruff and butch Bob, the mechanic and unlikely love interest for one of the three.

The shoot for the film took little over twenty-two days and they really did travel from Sydney to Alice Springs in that bus, it is true they did, well also a few other cars were needed too. Perhaps this method of film making along with the low budget of just under two million Aussie dollars that gives it the authentic camaraderie of that exists between a group of friends going through a physical and emotional journey. It has been an ultimate feel good film with a heart and soul, Elliott still gets fan and thank you letters, detailing how the film has changed the lives of people from all around the world. A stage musical version of the film opened in Sydney in 2006 and there have been productions in Melbourne, Auckland, London, Toronto, New York, Milan and Brazil have won a string of awards mainly best actors and best costume designs.

Priscilla is a beautiful magical combination of humour, catty bitchiness, kitsch costumes, stunning disco soundtrack and subtle sentiment with provocative thoughtful scenes and a delicate brush of honesty. Some jokes are obvious so too is the stereotypical veneer of the characters upon first glance, yet look a little deep as the film rolls on, you see more and more layers being unpeeled and exposed in a gently moving and comical way. It is one of the most enjoyable gay movies of all time; each subsequent viewing cements that sentiment further into fact.

"I love Adventures of Priscilla, Queen of the Desert. I think it's the best gay film I have ever seen. It offers everything, hilariously funny, incredibly bitchy, touchingly sad and so entertaining" **Alexander, Paris.**

"Simply for the reach and success outside the gay audience, Priscilla has to rate high in your quest for the most influential gay films. The mainstream audience made this a box office smash all over the world" **Andy, London.**

2

Brokeback Mountain

Director: Ang Lee

Starring: Jake Gyllenhaal, Health Ledger, Michelle Williams, Anne Hathaway.

From Academy Award-winning filmmaker Ang Lee comes the epic, Brokeback Mountain, the gay cowboy film. Many claimed this to be the archetypal all American love story, the only difference was that it was about two guys falling in love. Whilst that is true, it is a love story at its heart, it is also much more than that, it is an epic exploration of the complexities and difficulties of male love and social expectations in 1960's wild America.

Wyoming's beautiful vistas and wild countryside plays host to two young man who come together for work, yet end up falling in love with each other and form a lifelong relationship of many different layers.

It is the start of summer 1963; Ennis Del Mar meets Jack Twist as they wait to get jobs as ranch hands looking after sheep on Brokeback Mountain. From the moment, we first see them we can see they look the part of typical macho cowboys, all denim, big hats and long silent looks. Obviously, it helps that they are both rather pleasant to look at as is the wonderful Wyoming scenery, which really is Canadian scenery, but we will not quibble on that score. I would even go as far as saying that the scenery is the main lead and un-credited star of the movie, such is the ever-present natural magnificence.

Both come from rough backgrounds, they slowly start to bond by the campfire between the long hours of guarding sheep. It is interesting to watch the different personalities of the two gentlemen start to develop, grow and mature. A slightly drunken cold night leads to a rough and speechless animalistic coupling which for Ennis raises more questions than answers, although for Jack it seems to be the much needed connection he'd been seeking for many a long while.

The first part of the movie is relatively light on dialogue; the scenery and visual action do most of the story telling along with a deeply atmospheric score. Some of the best few lines of the first third come a day or so after their first rough shag, "This is a one shot thing we got going on here." Ennis says, "It's nobody's business but ours," replies Jack, they're both avoiding each other's eyes "You know I aint queer" confirms Ennis deliberately. "Me neither" offers Jack, it is both poignant, touching and yet tenderly speckles with affection, few words, yet they tell volumes for the feelings of those two men on the mountain. Then comes a wonderfully gentle and delightfully played love scene in the tent, gentle, caring, loving, honest, whilst they may be a little clumsy with each other, their affection is muscularly authentic and honest.

The summer comes to a premature end and Ennis and jack part their ways, Ennis married the pretty Alma, played exquisitely by Michelle Williams and life in the wild country goes on, including having twins. Jack turns his attentions back to rodeo fun, which he doesn't really excel at, however it leads him to meet the his future wife, rodeo riding, Lureen, Anne Hathaway. It should be happy every after for both these couples, children come and children grew, but there is trouble in the paradise of the north.

It is some four years later they meet again, with a rough, powerful, forceful kiss accidently spotted by Ennis' wife and the love the two cowboys had for each other ignites again, they spend the night in a cheap motel. They find each other again, but what does the future hold, they both have responsibilities but they both have needs, desires and longings. Jack wants to settle down with Ennis, he wants the little ranch where they could be together, happy, but Ennis is scared, two men living together, won't work, not in the place they live, not in the state they live, no, two men living together just is not a viable option. As soon as the words are said aloud, you instantly feel them tugging at your hearts strings for all there worth, it is almost painful.

A couple of times a year they get together for a 'fishing' trip, it isn't enough, they both know that in their heart of hearts, but it's all they can manage. Something has to give, something has to break and it could just be their hearts. The sadness plays to magnificent levels when Ennis has a postcard he sent to Jack returned with a big red 'Deceased' stamped across it, a painful telephone conversation with Jack's wife follows. The shocking details of what really happened and what they say what happened are played out in such horrendously vivid ways tears are libel to stream from already moist eyes.

Those eyes don't dry with the next scene of Ennis visiting Jacks folks, which says so much without words, the knowing, is everything. Finding Jack's shirt with Ennis' blood on the sleeve from their summer on Brokeback is a poignant reminder of a life once lived, of a happiness once shared. Seeing the shirts again in closet at the end with a postcard of Brokeback smacks of rich symbolism it is positively painful.

Brokeback Mountain was an exquisitely shot movie with such powerful sweeping cinematography and subtle intuitive directing from Ang Lee that it should be seen as a teaching guide on how to make a good motion picture. Incidentally, those two shirts went on to sell for $101,100 in a charity eBay auction.

One of the key issues of the many raised by Brokeback Mountain was the persecution and discrimination gay people faced in America in the 1960's when the story was based. However, the same kind of discrimination was evident in the many controversial incidents and defamatory hateful reporting of the movie but the American media particularly that of the Murdoch owned poisonous Fox network. Christian groups hated it, some tried to get it banned and some even picketed cinemas showing the film.

It went on to win a whole room full of awards, including three Oscars, four BAFTA's, four Golden Globes. It made over an approximate £112 million at the box offices worldwide and shifted more than 1.5 million DVD copies on its very first day of release in that format. The book, short story version also sold well and to my mind, the book was that much better. Brokeback achieved many things, not least making a gay love story popular with the mainstream heterosexual audience, which takes some doing. Many of my gay friends wondered what all the fuss was about at the time, perhaps because we had already lived through half a life facing discrimination and prejudice. Whilst my straight friends raved about it morning, noon and night, maybe because this was the first accessible film to highlight that being gay is not always easy and not every queer is as camp as Alan Carr or Graham Norton.

"Brokeback Mountain is one of the greatest tragic love stories ever told" **Christopher, Portslade.**

"Love, regret, wasted lives. Brokeback Mountain has it all." **Jess, Norwich.**

"I am not ashamed to say I cried buckets at the cinema, which for me is a first, very few films make me cry. It was a deeply moving film, incredibly sad, it was way more than the gay cowboy movie. It was a complex love story, between people with many layers, just like real life." **Dennis, Dorset.**

"Brokeback Mountain' a film which I liked a great deal more than some, I get irritated by a number of people who say that it was just an ordinary romance with two men instead of M/F. Really? Since when did a man and woman, after sex, deny that they were really heterosexual? When was the last time a gay gang beat another man to death because he was heterosexual? And all those eloquent silences between the men and their respective family members, because there was no vocabulary which would enable anyone to even dare to voice suspicions of such an unacceptable relationship, Ang Lee depicted so well with such acute observation. I thought it was a very fine film indeed and one of the very best 'gay' films to date." **Ray, Worthing.**

"Really loved Brokeback the book is better, though they're trying to convey very different things." **Anne Brooke, Author, Surrey.**

1

Philadelphia

Director: Jonathan Demme.

Starring: Tom Hanks, Denzel Washington.

If you were to ask anyone to name a Hollywood movie about AIDS the chances are they will give you a one word answer – Philadelphia. This Academy award-winning motion picture was one of the very first major mainstream Hollywood movies to not only acknowledge but also tackle head on the tragedy and discrimination people with HIV/AIDS had to endure on a daily basis. It transcended normal boundaries associated with a film about a disease, focusing less on the actual illness and more on the discrimination, prejudice and hostility that living with that disease attracts. Nevertheless, it goes way beyond that, it was a powerful piece of drama that opened up the subject of homophobia and AIDSophobia to a wide mass audience; it is also a commanding film about love.

It was a film born from the all too common misconceptions surrounding HIV / AIDS when it first emerged into society in the early and mid-1980's. There was a lot of fear surrounding the illness, people did not know how you contracted the disease, wild stories appeared in newspapers that even now would be scandalous and incendiary. One thing most people were sure of though, and that was they didn't want HIV/AIDS coming into their homes, their children's schools, the diner on the corner where they got coffee, in the park where they might walk pouchy and most definitely not their workplace.

The primary population of those contracting this new and savagely resistant illness was primarily gay males, who by and large were still, and in some places, still are, an ostracised part of society. There was a lot of aggression and disregard to the gay population at the birth of the onslaught of an epidemic that had no known cure. This discrimination, prejudice and hatred ran up from the general homophobe in the streets right up all the way to the top echelons of governments.

Philadelphia was also one of the first mainstream Hollywood movies that featured gay characters that were not murders, freaky villains, or stereotypical camp buffoons, which for many was a true revelations and as pivotal and the main subject matter itself. The producers also went to great lengths to invite as many gay actors and people living with AIDS to play extra and walk on parts in the movie which not only adds to the authentic look of the film, but also the incredibly personal feel that was extraordinarily poignant. Heartbreakingly, many of those actors were not around to see movie premiered on the big screen.

The fact that the story of Philadelphia was loosely based upon the real events of Geoffrey Bowers, a gay attorney who sued law firm Baker & McKenzie in 1987 adds a touch more gravitas on the movie, which is sometimes often overlooked. Especially from within the gay community who were, it has to be said pretty divided about the film upon its release in 1993/94 and even to this day regarding the validity, power, influence, accuracy and success of the movie.

The opening stirrings of Bruce Springstien's Streets of Philadelphia over moving images that have nothing to do with the film, yet everything to do with Philadelphia, pull at the our consciousness from the very outset. You know this is not going to be your ordinary 'happy and glossy' Hollywood flick, such is the ominous and depressingly sad feeling it evokes proves it justly deserved winning the Academy award for best original song.

The first real or dramatic scene is between the two central characters, Andrew Beckett and Joe Miller, two lawyers fighting each other, whose relationship evolves throughout the movie, is one of the main appeals for much of the audience. Then comes a brief hospital scene, which blasts the comfort of the homophobe audience out of the water with visions of real people with AIDS in what is amazingly commanding and indicative of what the film is about.

The ability of Beckett as a lawyer is made clear by the high regard he's held in within the law firm, the offices of which look incredibly swish and modern and it's fairly clear this the home of one of the most prestigious law firms in Philadelphia. Beckett is a senior associate and a rising star, he has given a prestigious case, however one of the partners notices a little bruise on Beckett's forehead, which the young lawyer passes off as the mark of a wayward racket ball.

The next scene quickly establishes, if any of the audience is in any doubt, the mark on Beckett's head is so not a bruise but a lesion. A trademark lesion of Kaposi Sarcoma an opportunistic illness of particular prevalence among people with AIDS, it is also an illness that goes on to play a major part in the upcoming court case. However, because of this, Beckett has to work from home and we see a touching attempt to cover the lesion with make-up, which no doubt strikes a chord with many the world over.

The big complaint that Beckett was given seems to go missing, despite we, the audience see Beckett place it on the desk in the dead of night. The niceness of the character is ably demonstrated by the fact that he knows the night security guard by name, enforcing the likeability of the character and the care, we the audience already feel for him. Yet it is this missing document that causes the young and gifted lawyer to be sacked from the firm by the partners that used to refer to him as buddy and saw him as somewhat of a star protégé.

The action fast-forwards a month and we see the re-emergence of the other main central character, Joe Miller, his wife has just had a baby the lawyer is glowing from ear to ear. Beckett is not doing so well, he has asked several attorneys to take on his case before he shows us at Miller's office. There follows a key scene between the two trading on their situations and prejudices which is so wonderfully played and shot it feels like a sharp dig in the ribs forcing emotions to the forefront of our collective minds, tears are so close to the surface.

It is obvious that Miller is your run of the mill usual homophobic heterosexual male who is ignorant of the facts surround AIDS, hammered home by a visit Miller makes to his family doctor and his discussions with his wife at home, which are truly offensive, yet exactly what the homophobic audience members are thinking.

Beckett is unable to find a lawyer willing or brave enough to take on the case, thus has no option other than trying the case himself, he starts his research in the library. Miller watches from a distance as a little confrontation between librarian and Beckett takes place which highlights the discrimination, revulsion and prejudice people with HIV/AIDS were often subjected to, although this is a mild 'Hollywood' softening version, it is still potent enough to cause a stabbing pain in our sensibilities. Miller, sees enough and comes over to intercede and cut an awkward situation, at first he is hesitant, but relents, his interest is piqued, he sits and Beckett starts to explain his case, in basic details, which includes the painful reading of a ruling of law that hammers home the ultimate and hitherto unspoken yet realised culmination of the story. "Although the ruling did not specify the issue of HIV and AIDS discrimination, subsequent decisions have held that AIDS is a protected as a handicap under law, not only because of the physical limitations it imposes but because the prejudices surrounding AIDS, exacts a social death that proceeds the actual physical one."

The papers are served, scenes follow that show the bad guys conspiring and being nasty, the way bad guys do. Then the good guys having a good time and showing the support of a strong family. Perhaps the family scene are a little heavily laden with sentimentality but still help the story along and given an insight into the inner strength the character Beckett has.

Then we are in the court, the whole three quarters of an hour have been building up to this moment, this is bread and butter of the film, the inner core. It is during this opening court scene that Denzel Washington really excels as the lawyer with prejudices, Joe Miller and lights up the screen with a passion and a power that is truly remarkable.

Many issues are bought painfully to the surface during the trial scenes and those surrounding them, which are sometimes hard to face up to, yet we as a society watched them take place and were, in some cases even guilty of. It focuses on the individual characters and their thoughts, their feelings their insecurities and prejudices which make this such a human film. There are delightful touches of comedy paced throughout the impressive dialogue, which lift the sombre subject matter in subtle and sometime unsubtle ways.

The party scene is intercedes the court action and for many this is the most controversial scene, some love it and some hate it. For me it is an amusing entertaining scene, which although purports to be just a fancy dress part is actually a memorial gathering or wake for the living. It is well put together technically with fluid moving shots, great lighting and numerous interesting background artists, including the 'legendary gay' Quieten Crisp. There is a famous anecdote that during a special screening for the President of the United States Of America at the White House, Bill Clinton got up to leave for the bathroom as soon as Beckett and his partner, both in brilliant white naval uniforms start to dance. A wonderful powerful moment that again is overlooked, for gays in the military was a key issue during this period, just before or just after Don't Ask, Don't Tell had just been passed. Raising the issue of equality in US military, which has only recently been resolved.

The opera scene, which comes next, is often talked about, many love it, and many hate it, telling the two sides of a stereotype. A Gay man loving opera so much that it moves him to tears and he just has to tell others of the deep emotion the music evokes and explores and celebrates. The jury is still out on the validity and purpose of it, but, for me it works so very well, it's also incredibly well shot and makes a lovely break from the heart wrenching story unfolding in the courtroom scenes. However, is gay people enjoying the beauty and majesty of deeply emotive opera music really a bad stereotype to portray?

The following scenes of Beckett on the stand are deeply controversial yet unbelievably mightily impassioned and tremendously telling. I can still hear the audible gasps I heard during the London release of the film when Beckett opens his shirt to reveal the KS lesions, a collective moment of caring and shock for the character. The look he gives Miller straight after is one of shame, humiliation and yet supreme thanks and admiration.

The collapse of Andrew Beckett in the courtroom is, to be honest rather expected and anticipated, yet even so, it is still violently distressingly poignant that is hard to watch without feeling the slightest bit of emotion. It looks and probably was painful and so dramatic without being over the top and gruesome. It leads the way to the case being won in Beckets absence which gives way to the inevitable hospital scene where were see the characters say good bye for one final time as well as the Miller character to evolve from his loathing of homosexuals and revulsion of AIDS to acceptance, care and respect.

The best and the worst scene follows of the wake, which relied heavily on the raw and tumultuous emotions that such a story conjures up and plays with in such blatant fashion. Is it overly emotional too sentimental as we journey from the gathered friends and family to the beautifully shot grainy home movies purporting to be of Beckett as a small boy, over the top plays the superb Neil Young number Philadelphia and the journey is complete.

Philadelphia remains one of the greatest and most successful gay themed movies so far in the history of cinema; its message still rings true even now, as we approach its twentieth anniversary. There will be few who can forget the incredible performance from Tom Hanks as the brilliant yet discriminated against HIV positive layer Andy Beckett, whom justly won the Oscar for best actor of 1993. It was a triumphant heart achingly authentic portrayal of someone stuck down by this debilitating and devastating disease. For the bulk of the film he is so far removed from the average Joe next door that it is possible to be, deathly thin and emaciated, head shaved and sallow skinned this guy really took some punishment for this part. I can only salute Tom's ability to cut through some of the crap and give us a powerfully positive and honourable gay character to be proud of up there on the big Hollywood screen.

All credit to Denzel Washington too, for his portrayal of the homophobe with a heart, Joe Miller, the money grabbing, ambulance chasing lawyer whose ethics may at times be a little suspect, but play out good in the end. There were times in the movie that I certainly wanted to give him a piece of my mind or the back of my hand, which only goes to further illustrate the wonderful believability of his acting style and strength.

Philadelphia is an unendingly compassionate and compelling film, which also pulled in a vast amount of criticism for putting a pretty face on AIDS, for being so far removed from the real world it might as well have come from Pluto. The Washington Post went so far as to say it was so far and so much like propaganda it made Nazi documentaries looking like super 8 home movies. A safe sex kind of movie, so far removing you from the actual issue, yet congratulating you for talking about it. They called it a toothless wonder, campaigned for poor ticket sales and told you it should have stayed on the back seat of the bus. They were not alone, many many people slated it, especially so called enlightened folk from the gay community, who deemed it too soft, too pure and too easy going on the harsh realities of AIDS. Yet, had it been harsher, grittier, more physically gruelling to watch, would it have been seen by such large audience numbers, or would it have been watched and endured by just the gay community, as with most other gay / AIDS movies? Preaching to the converted does not do anything to embraces, inform and entertain the mainstream, no matter how glossy or not it happens to be. Preaching to the converted does not get more followers and preaching to the converted does not raise much more awareness. Many complained about the lack of physical love between the lead gay characters, there are few tender moments between them and perhaps, I would have liked to have seen a little more emotion and contact, this really was not a movie about their relationship and about gay sex as such, it was deeper and more powerful than that. It had a tremendous reach, with an estimated gross at the box office of around £130 million worldwide, proved that it wasn't just preaching to the converted, either that or there are a lot more gays in the village than we ever thought.

What is amazing and indicates the influential impact Philadelphia had is that we're still talking about it in impassioned ways and it is still the most famous and most successful gay AIDS movies out there, almost a full twenty years from its release.

"Philadelphia is truly a tremendous movie" **Simon, London.**

"Without Philadelphia I may never have come out at work, it hold such a special place in my heart." **Andy, Sussex.**

"On paper Philadelphia should have been a big flop, Silence of the Lambs director directs the star of Big on a film about gays and AIDS in the early 90's in which the end is the death. Plus he didn't get AIDS in a nice movie way like a blood transfusion, he got it in a porn movie cinema having random nameless sex. Yet he took America and the world by the balls and gave them a damn good pulling. It changed lives, it honestly did, it made sleepy middle America more compassionate and perhaps accepting of gay people and AIDS." **Sam, Illinois.**

"I'm not sure about influential, but I loved, loved, loved Philadelphia, it is one of my favorites." **Becca, Florida.**

"It grossed something like $210 million, name any other gay film that has done that. That is influential." **Anon**

Not exactly how you would have voted, or you have suggested an alternative influential gay movie, well you can always have your say and nominate your choice for the next edition – email gaymovies@seafrontdiary.com

Sorry, but we will not be able to send you a personal reply regarding your nomination, however your words may be used as quotes in the next edition, so please include your town or city with your email. Thank you.